Opal Whiteley

The Continuing Mystery

Elizabeth Lawrence

Thomas Harmsworth Publishing Company

First Published 2000 by
Thomas Harmsworth Publishing Company
Old Rectory Offices
Stoke Abbott
Beaminster
Dorset DT8 3JT
United Kingdom

British Library Cataloguing-in-Publication Data. A catalogue record for this book is available from the British Library.

ISBN 0 948807 49 0

Printed and bound in Great Britain by
Bookcraft, Midsomer Norton, Bath.

Dedication

to my many friends who have encouraged me
in the long pursuit of the truth about Opal,
especially Robert Lindsey Nassif,
whose friendship with and belief in Françoise has never faltered; and Rosalie Lulham who first told me about the *Diary* more than sixty years ago.

Acknowledgements and thanks

Every attempt has been made to obtain copyright permission for quotations and illustrations.

Acknowledgements are offered to the following:
Richard, Lord Acton
Jeff Burnham
Inez Fortt
Constant Huntington
London University Library
Andrew Meltzoff
Robert Lindsey Nassif
Old Oregon, now *Oregon Quarterly*
Ellery Sedgwick
Steve Williamson
Hon. Mrs Woodruff

The distinguished psychologist, John Flavell, once told us he would trade all of his awards for the chance to see through a child's eyes for just a few minutes. The early nineteenth-century Romantic poets, such as Wordsworth and Blake, had the same ambition. They thought childhood was the time when we saw the universe most clearly. It was 'a time when meadow, grove and stream, the earth, and every common sight, to me did seem apparelled in celestial light.' The time when we saw 'a world in a grain of sand and heaven in a wild flower.'

Andrew Meltzoff: *How Babies Think.*

Introduction

The mystery of this haunting Diary is still unsolved. Said to be the work of a young child, brought up in the forests of Oregon, it has been the centre of controversy for over seventy years.

The *Daily Express* of September 1962 reported*

'In 1919 a hat box was despatched from California to the office of the *Atlantic Monthly.* It contained the torn diary of Opal Whiteley. It was written in coloured chalk on shreds of paper and its author set about piecing it together. The result was an extraordinary book called *The Diary of Opal Whiteley.* It is set in the Oregon woods and contains the essence of what is real to a child — walks, trees, castor oil and punishment.'

Naomi Lewis wrote in the *Sunday Observer,* also in September 1962:

'It is a puzzling tale in which every doubt appears to have an element of fact, and every fact, an element of doubt. If the diary is not the immediate work of a child, it is, certainly the work of someone remembering with absolute clarity the sensation of being a child. I find it a moving document.'

But this is not all.

The diary was barely published before Opal was claiming that her name was not Opal but Françoise, and that her father was not Ed Whiteley, but no other than Prince Henry of Orleans, the pretender to the throne of France.

The mystery is still there, but the importance of the diary

does not consist in who its author was. Its value lies in the insight it gives into the inner life of childhood, that inner life so much forgotten by the adult world and whose existence and influence we neglect at our peril.

* Edna O'Brien.

1.

In March 1992 a remarkable funeral took place in the heart of London, in the oldest Catholic Church in England.

A handful of people, in ones and twos, came quietly into the beautiful church of St Ethelreda. The sun shone through the brilliant stained glass of the windows and from the gallery came the sound of a choir singing Gregorian chants. A small coffin, almost buried in white lilies, lay in front of the altar. The priest entered and began intoning the latin mass. A team of television photographers moved quietly about, filming the whole ceremony.

In the small congregation was a Member of the English House of Lords; the daughter of an English peer, widow of the one time editor of the leading Catholic newspaper, *The Tablet;* a Professor of Oriental Studies from the University of Cambridge; an American author and teacher of Law Studies in a midwest University; the Official Solicitor of the Court of Protection and three of the nurses who had cared for the deceased in her last years. Surely this must be the funeral of some famous and distinguished person.

A member of the congregation stepped forward to the lectern and began to read:

'I wonder if honeysuckles grow about the gates of Heaven. I've heard they are made of precious jewels. I have thinks there will be flowers growing all about. Probably God brought the seed from heaven when he did plant the flowers here on earth.

Too, I do think when angels bring babies from heaven to folks that live here below, they do also bring seeds of flowers and do scatter them about. I have thinks that they do this so the babies may hear the voices of the loving flowers and grow in the ways of God.'

The reading was from the *Diary of Opal Whiteley,* a book published originally in America in 1922 and said to be the work of a child. The church where the ceremony was taking place was one in which Opal herself had worshipped when, as an adult, she came to London. I was the reader.

It was 60 years since I had first read the *Diary* and thirty years since the publication of my book, *Opal Whiteley, the Unsolved Mystery.* Now this was the last that the world would see of this hauntingly fascinating personality, for this was the funeral of Opal Whiteley, or, as the London *Times* styled her in the Obituary column, Françoise Marie de Bourbon-Orléans.

Those few of us there that day, all of whom had known her in some way and loved her *Diary,* felt that it was just as she would have wished it to be.

From the church we accompanied her to the prestigious cemetery at Highgate, resting place of many of England's famous dead — and Karl Marx — and closed for years to any more burials; but here a corner had been found for this obscure American from the lumber country of Oregon, and, with full Catholic rites and filmed by television, she was laid to rest in the strangely haunted cemetery, closely packed with old gravestones, obelisks and pyramids of angels, all grown over with ivy and creeper.

So ended a story begun nearly a hundred years ago in the forests of Oregon, which, in that time had moved readers all over the world; stirred up controversy in the world of literature; opened the minds of many to the importance of the inner life of childhood; inspired an American to write and produce a musical play in New York, which the *New York Times* said 'drew one into a place of magical transformations.'

The story of Opal has not died away. Interest in this strange child seems to have no end. The mystery remains and may never be solved: but in the thirty years since the publication of *Opal Whiteley — The Unsolved Mystery* some parts of the jigsaw have been found and fitted.

When the *Diary* was first published in London, England, the Chairman of the Company who published it, wrote, 'The whole of Fleet Street is absorbed in this book.'

The appearance of the *Diary* was indeed a unique event in the world of literature and raised a whirlwind of interest, the last eddies of which have not yet died away. Overnight the author found herself in a position of controversy such as few have occupied in literature or history.

The *Diary* had originally appeared in serial form in the American journal, the *Atlantic Monthly,* where it bore the title *The Journal of an Understanding Heart.* It was claimed to be the work of a child, written in her sixth or seventh years. Its publication had the effect of a minor explosion in the literary world. Letters of appreciation, bearing the signatures of men of letters and of science, poured into the offices of the *Atlantic.* Newspapers in America and England carried reviews. In a short time the first part, *The Journal,* appeared as a book, about which the majority of critics were not only favourable, but enthusiastic in their praise.

The *New York Times* said, 'All who wish to understand childhood, all who wish to find joy in it will do well to read this *Journal of an Understanding Heart.* It is a wonderful book.'

Christopher Morley, writing in *The New York Evening Post* said, 'That it is a beautiful and touching and piercingly honest revelation of an imaginative child's spirit seems to me to be evident beyond cavil.'

'Every true lover of children will read it spellbound,' said *The Daily Telegraph,* 'and the reader who fails to respond to its appeal has surely lost the secret of his own childhood.'

'A book full of beauty and equally full of meaning, a fascinating picture of the child mind,' wrote *The Observer* and the London *Times* said, 'Opal Whiteley is a child St Francis in the joyousness that pervades her in the midst of the pain she shares and strives to alleviate; and her passionate sympathy with all nature — animate and inanimate — is that of the Saint who preached to the birds and fishes, and summoned Sister Moon, Brother Wind and Sister Water to praise God. We hope that Opal Whiteley will write the other books she planned in childhood, but we do not expect them to be like this book; it is one of those inspirations which can seldom be repeated.'

The Morning Post said, 'Even if the touch of mystery were lacking, the utter simplicity of the child's observations would make it one of the most entrancing books that were ever printed.'

'The touch of mystery' was to grow more compelling and fascinating as the years went on.

A small minority showed some scepticism, but the majority recognised the *Diary* as not only completely genuine, but as the work of an astonishing genius.

The Times Literary Supplement wrote, 'One is inclined to say that her book is the most complete picture of a child's inner life that can be imagined,' and *The New York World* said, 'The story of Opal is one of the most striking human documents of the times. It promises quite to eclipse other recent presentments of childhood precocity, possessing as it does, along with the evidence of a lively fancy, the quality of a genuine, unthinking revelation of a sharply sensitive self.'

The Chairman of the firm that published the book in England, Putnam & Company, wrote in December 1920, 'We consider it one of the most attractive and important books which we have ever published,' and again in April 1921, 'I feel very strongly that it will be a great and serious loss to the world if the whole of the *Diary* is not published. Miss Whiteley's books are not a matter of a season's interest. I regard the *Diary* as a very remarkable work of genius, ranking with the great works of all time.' Praise indeed!

The journal attracted attention not only by its revelation of a remarkable child with a unique power of expression, but by the strange circumstances of its publication. The manuscript was in thousands of pieces, some the size of a postage stamp, some as large as a half sheet of note paper, and had to be pieced together like a vast jig-saw puzzle. It was written in coloured pencils, on odd pieces of brown wrapping paper, butchers' bags, the backs of envelopes, on anything that was available. Opal, who was twenty-two when the *Diary* was published, herself carried out the work of sorting the thousands of pieces to prepare the manuscript for publication, a task that took her nine months of continuous work.

One quotation from the *Diary* will give an idea of its remarkable quality and Opal's almost Swinburnian use of words. She is describing how she helped to lift the potatoes in the family vegetable patch:

'And all the time I was picking up potatoes I did have conversations with them. Too, I did have thinks of all their growing days there in the ground, and all the things they did hear. Earth-voices are glad voices, and earth-songs come up from the ground through the plants; and in their flowering and in the days before these days are come, they do tell the earth-songs to the wind. And the wind in her goings does whisper them to folks to print for other folks. So other folks do have knowing of earth's songs.

I have thinks these potatoes growing here did have knowings of star-songs. I have kept watch in the fields at night and I have seen the stars look kindness down upon them. And I have walked between the rows of potatoes and I have watched the star-gleam on their leaves. And I have heard the wind ask of them the star-songs the star-gleams did tell in shadows on their leaves. And as the wind did go walking in the field talking to the earth-voices there, I did follow her down the rows. I did have feels of her presence near.'

An introduction to the *Diary* was contributed by Viscount Grey of Falloden, one time English ambassador in Washington. He met Opal at the *Atlantic* office and was deeply impressed by her knowledge and understanding of nature. Of their first meeting Opal later wrote,

'It was one of the most thrilling days of my whole life for I discovered in Lord Grey a kindred soul, because he loved trees more than the walls of houses, and he spoke of listening to their sap going up in the Spring. He told me of his ducks at Falloden, and how when the mate of one died, though he bought another mate, the drake left alone would have nothing to say to her, but preferred his loneliness, and went away from the water at Falloden, which had been so long his home.'

(Why did this story makes so a great an impression on Opal? Her life was to follow a very similar pattern to that of the lonely drake.)

'And Lord Grey told me of his brother's pet pig in Africa, who would come to meet him like a dog, putting up his front feet on his master's knees.

On that memorable day Lord Grey gave me my first complete book of Wordsworth's poems. Until then I had possessed only selections, earned by picking blackberries in the lumber camps. That Christmas Lord Grey sent me two of W H Hudson's books, whose English style he thought it would be well for me to study.'

Of his impression of Opal, Lord Grey wrote, 'No-one who met her could help being impressed by her interest in all natural objects, which is as spontaneous and simple as it is vivid and intense. I have read her book with sheer delight.'

2.

Who was the child who claimed to have written the *Journal* at such an early age and who was buried with such ceremony after her death? No one is certain. At her funeral the priest had said 'I gather there was some doubt as to who this lady really was.' Her background is, and always has been, a mystery. The known facts are that she grew up, at least from the age of five or six in Oregon, in the family of a logger and his wife, Mr and Mrs Whiteley. The family was poor. Mr Whiteley was constantly moving from one mill to another and Mrs Whiteley was compelled to work at cooking and washing to keep the family. Relations between Mr and Mrs Whiteley were not always harmonious and for some of Opal's childhood at least, the two were separated. Since the family was constantly moving, Opal's education must have been patchy and interrupted.

In the spring of 1916 Opal went to Eugene, to attend a Christian Endeavor Convention. She spoke at the Convention and made a considerable impression. Shortly afterwards she was made State Junior Superintendent of Christian Endeavor and became well-known in the movement.

Her ambition was to be head of all Junior Endeavor work in Oregon. She said that she had been preparing herself for the position for some time, and her next ambition was to write nature books for children, books in which the miracle of life in the forest would be made clear and full of meaning.

She then went to College, to the University of Eugene. This was some distance from her home and to pay for her lodgings she worked as a house servant.

According to *The Call Number*, published by the Staff Association of the University of Oregon Library, Opal 'introduced herself to the University by presenting a rock specimen known as heulandite, previously unknown in the state. As a result, the professors of geology, the curator of the museum, the professors of science, all welcomed her, encouraged her to study and ask all the questions she wished. Her knowledge of geography, geology, botany and zoology astonished her hearers, and she was declared a child prodigy.

Questioned by the professors regarding her powers of concentration and her ability to memorise, Opal claimed that for mental discipline she recited the names of hundreds of specimens in her collections.'

She intended to earn a living by giving nature lessons and through her writing to teach children about God.

The University publication went on,

'Opal believed and demonstrated to her classes that the life cycle of a monarch butterfly was a divine symbol of immortality. Between sandwiches and pickles, the picnicking Juniors inspected caterpillars and tadpoles, found hummingbird eggs, and saw God in everything and heard Him in the wind. In a botany course at Cottage Grove High School in 1912, her beetles, moths, butterflies and birds took on meaning, identity and a sense of universal order. From Smithsonian Institution publications, books from the State Library and various government pamphlets, Opal filled seventeen copy books with quotations, notes, lists and identifications. Three thousand rock specimens were classified, and a record made of all insect and plant life in her growing collection.

The book she wrote for children, entitled *The Fairyland Around Us* contains photographs which she took herself, of some of the children in her classes. They are feeding young birds and have toads, birds and chipmunks in their hands. The expression on their faces testifies to the remarkable effect Opal's work and inspiration had on them. When I was in Oregon I met one of these children — then in her eighties — Mrs Lemon. She pointed to the photograph opposite page 109, in which she and a number of other children are giving the pledge of friendship to tree fairies.

She was accepted by the University in circumstances that testify to her unusual ability. She had none of the usual qualifications but all restrictions were laid aside and she was enrolled. 'In three days,' the *Eugene Guard* reported, 'she became the talk of the faculty of three educational institutions.' The head of the University Geological Department, Dr Warren D Smith, said, 'she knows more about geology than do many students that have graduated from my department. She may become one of the greatest minds Oregon has ever produced. She will be an investment for the University.'

She came to the University, 'tutored by nature,' as the *Guard* put it. A B Sweeter, head of the Botany Department called her 'a travesty on our educational system. Is all our great system wasted; is it hindering normal development?' he asked.

Dr Smith said, 'I never saw anyone so hungry for knowledge. She has enough energy and enthusiasm for a whole class.'

The Call went on, 'She spent much of her time filling fruit jars with butterflies and moths. Her capture of these specimens was a source of amazement on the campus, where the sight of the small, dark girl whizzing by in pursuit of game became quite common.'

Elizabeth Hales was a student in the same class as Opal. When I met her in Eugene at age 92, she told me;

'We were in one class together — palaeontology. She sat in the front row. The thing I remember about her she was so enthusiastic. After a while the instructor lectured only to her.'

She continued with her work for Junior Endeavor alongside

her nature studies. 'Posters invited one and all to hear Opal Whiteley, the remarkable girl naturalist who combined caterpillars and Christian Endeavor.

In the fall of 1916 Opal was officially on the campus of the University of Oregon, registered in the College of Literature Science and the Arts.'

A fellow student described her appearance at that time:

'She wore her hair long in dramatic streamers which hung down on either side. Her skirts were very short and full at a time when the rest of us were trying to appear grown-up with our hair up and our skirts long and narrow. While we minced across the campus in our narrow skirts and hopped over the open ditches where the sewers were being laid, Opal ran and jumped across, her hair streaming out behind her and her skirts billowing in the wind.'

Opal registered for courses in palaeontology, history, chemistry, ethics, English, and hockey, a total of sixteen and one half hours in today's terms, not including a course at Eugene Bible University.

For any ordinary student such a course load would have been enough, but to Opal the class work was something to do between spurts of activity in Christian Endeavor, and a self-improvement calendar that was as strenuous as it was unusual. Fortunately the Whiteley family had removed from Cottage Grove to Springfield, whence Opal commuted to the campus. At home she was surrounded by her collections and books.

The surviving volumes of Opal's library range from history to drama, and from art texts to catalogues of lepidoptera. As she once stated to an Oregonian reporter, 'every moment on this earth is too precious to waste,' and she followed her own advice by reading in the University library between classes, 'while the other students chat in the halls.'

Opal's energies were almost entirely directed towards the Junior Endeavor movement, to the detriment of her University studies. She was to attend the national convention of Christian Endeavor in New York in July 1917, but in May of that year both her grandmother and her mother died and this double blow ended both the plans for New York and her involvement in the movement.

Instead of going to New York she spent the summer travelling through Oregon giving lectures and lessons on nature for which pupils paid 10 cents. With the money she paid for a little house in which she would live while completing her studies at the University. In this she set up a collection of 16,000 specimens of natural history.

For her second year at University Opal registered courses in general geology, latin, art, dramatic interest, short story-writing and gym and a course in eugenics. This interested her particularly and she made notes about family traits and inherited characteristics and began to investigate the backgrounds of her own family members. On her [Angel] father's side she found a link with the name of Stanley, dating back to 1277 and discovered that one of the family had been the 17th Earl of Derby. She also made links with other noble English families: the Percys, the Staffords and the Harvards.

She explored the family tree of Philip the Bold, of Charles Valois and Philip VI of France, and the lineage of the De Vere family. She adopted some of these names for own, when she began to call herself Opal De Vere Gabrielle De Bourbon de la Tremouille Stanley Whiteley and she used some of them for the animals in *The Story of Opal.* There is a significant note amongst her papers, in her handwriting: 'To find out: year of birth, place of birth, parents.'

By the middle of her second year at the University she had run out of money and had earned only seven units of credit in the fall term. Her grandmother tried to get her a teaching job but Opal had other plans. She withdrew from University, intending to go to California to do research work and lecturing, but in fact her ambition was to get into Hollywood, but this came to nothing.

In one of the periodicals in her own library there was an article which she had marked. Seen in the context of her own life it has perhaps great significance. It was entitled *Imagination, the greatest faculty in man.* 'The power of imagination,' it said, 'can set in motion currents that will be so powerful that they will actually force us into situations in the real that we previously pictured in imagination.' In her notebook Opal wrote,

'Our imagination is the instrument of reality. By means of it we are brought face-to-face with the past, and by means of it we prophesy the future.' Was she aware of this power and of her own ability to wield it, even at this early stage of her life?

She had already begun writing a book for children, the purpose of which was to teach them about God by means of stories of His creatures — plant, animal and bird. This book, called *The Fairyland Around Us* was eventually published at her own expense in Los Angeles. Some difficulty arose with the publisher and Opal, sadly out of pocket over her expensive attempt, tried to find another publisher to take over the publication.

With the characteristic assurance she had shown in leading the Christian Endeavor Movement, she had no hesitation in writing to the Great to recommend her book. She sent the early chapters to Theodore Roosevelt, telling him she had advance orders from the Queen of the Belgians and King George V of England. Eventually she brought the book to the office of the *Atlantic Monthly.* The editor, Ellery Sedgwick, described what took place on this occasion and the impression that Opal made on him.

'Late on an afternoon in September, Opal Whiteley came into the *Atlantic's* office with a book which she had had printed in Los Angeles. The book was quaintly embellished with coloured pictures, pasted in by hand, and bore a hundred marks of special loving care. Yet about it there seemed little to tempt a publisher. But about Opal Whiteley herself there was something to attract the attention even of a man of business — something very young and eager and fluttering, like a bird in a thicket.

The talk went as follows:

'I am afraid we can't do anything with the book. But you must have had an interesting life. You have lived much in the woods?'

'Yes, in lots of lumber camps.'

'How many?'

'Nineteen. At least we moved nineteen times.'

One close question followed another regarding the surroundings of her girlhood. The answers were so detailed, so sharply remembered, that the next question was natural.

'If you remember like that, you must have kept a diary.'

Her eyes opened wide. 'Yes, always. I do still.'

'Then it is not this book I want, but the diary.'

She caught her breath. 'It's destroyed. It's all torn up.' Tears were in her eyes.

'You loved it?'

'Yes, I told it everything.'

'Then you kept the pieces?'

The guess was easy. What child whose doll is rent asunder throws away the sawdust? But she looked amazed.

'Yes, I have kept everything. The pieces are all stored in Los Angeles.'

We telegraphed for them, and they came, crammed in a hatbox: hundreds, thousands, one might say half a million of them. Some few were large as a half sheet of note paper; more, scarce big enough to hold a letter of the alphabet. The paper was of all shades, sorts, and sizes; butchers' bags pressed and sliced in two, wrapping paper, backs of envelopes — anything and everything that could hold writing. The early years of the diary are printed in letters so close that, when sheets are fitted, not another letter can be squeezed in.

In later passages the characters are written with childish

clumsiness, and later still, one sees the gradually forming adult hand. The labour of piecing the diary together may fairly be described as enormous. For nine months, almost continuously, the diarist had laboured, piecing it together sheet by sheet, each page a kind of picture puzzle, lettered, for frugality (the store was precious) on both sides of the paper.'*

While Opal was engaged on this task, she lived in the home of Sedgwick's mother-in-law, Mrs Walter C Cabot, as one of the family. As each sheet was fitted together, and could be read, it was typed out, only the spelling and punctuation being altered, and in March 1920 it began to be published, as a series of articles in the *Atlantic Monthly.* A few months later the New York firm of Putnam published it as a book, with a preface written by Ellery Sedgwick.

Some parts, where it was impossible to fit the torn scraps together, had to be omitted, and the names of some of the less important characters were changed to prevent identification. Apart from these, no changes were made, except for, as Ellery Sedgwick put it, in the preface.

'Adult rules of capitalisation and punctuation, of which the manuscript is absolutely innocent, were adopted. The spelling, with the exception of occasional characteristic examples of the diarist's individual style, has been amended, lest the journal seem precious, rather than beautifully natural and interpretative of the spirit of childhood.'

* *The Happy Profession,* Ellery Sedgwick. Eyre & Spottiswoode, 1948.

3.

The publication in the the *Atlantic Monthly* brought Opal immediate fame and publicity. Letters of appreciation came from all parts of the USA. One of these proved to be the opening for employment in the next years of her life:

'My Dear Miss Whiteley,

Perhaps it is a presumption on my part to address you, and to think that you may give me even a moment's attention, and yet I cannot resist at least trying to approach you, and to ask your help on a matter that is very close to my heart. I have two children, one a boy of nearly twelve; the other a girl, named H..., aged just thirteen. H... has always had an interest in nature and animals. My great desire is that this tendency in H... shall have encouragement and that she may come in closer touch with this big part of life in a natural, wholesome, reverent manner.

As *The Journal of an Understanding Heart* presents a person with such beautiful, rare understanding, I cannot help but make the attempt to secure from her a little help in my problem. I would love to take more of your time to tell you the joy and deep inspiration that we, as a family, have received from 'The Story of Opal.' It is with great eagerness that I shall be looking for a response from you.'

The request was that Opal should take on the education of the two children, and this led to her employment in this and other families.

The first suggestion that there was some mystery about Opal's origin appeared at the time of the publication of the *Diary.* Without any preliminary hints she began to make the claim that she was not the child of Mr and Mrs Whiteley. Her story was that she had been substituted, before the age of five, for another child and given her name.

It appeared that some time during 1902 Mrs Whiteley had left her husband to go on a visit to her mother at Wendling, Oregon, taking her two children with her. The elder of them was then aged about five. Wendling was about 350 miles distant and Mrs Whiteley and the children stayed at Portland on the way.

How long they remained there is unknown, or what, if anything, took place, but it was Opal's belief that on this journey she was exchanged for Mrs Whiteley's elder child, also named Opal. It was reported in later years that Mrs Whiteley would never go to Portland and could not bear even to hear the name mentioned.

In the preface to the *Diary* Ellery Sedgwick wrote,

'Opal Whiteley was born about twenty-two years ago, where, we have no knowledge. Of her parents, whom she lost before her fifth year, she is sure of nothing except that they loved her, and that she loved them with a tenacity of affection as strong now as at the time of parting. To recall what manner of people they were, no physical proof remains, except, perhaps, two precious little copybooks, which held their photographs and wherein her mother and father had set down things which they wished their little daughter to learn, both of the world about her and of that older world of legend and history, with which the diarist shows such capricious and entertaining familiarity. These books, for reasons beyond her knowledge, were taken away from Opal when she was about twelve years of age, and have never been returned, although there is ground for believing that they are still in existence.'

Here and there in the *Diary* one comes across references to two people, spoken of as Angel Father and Angel Mother, whom Opal clearly believed to be her true parents:

'We went on along the dim trail. There by the dim trail grow the honeysuckles. I nod to them as I go that way. In the daytime I hear them talk with sunbeams and the wind. They talk in shadows with the little people of the sun. And this I have learned — grown ups do not know the language of shadows. Angel Mother and Angel Father did know and they taught me. I wish they were here now — here to listen with me. I do so want them. Sometimes they do seem near. I have thinks kind God just opens the gates of heaven and lets them come out to be guardian angels for a little while.'

Opal writes of how her Angel Father told her the names of insects and flowers and birds and of a game he taught her, which she calls 'comparer:'

'I did hurry away in the way that does lead to the house of the girl that has no seeing. She does so like to feel things. She has seeing by feels. And too I tell her about comparer, that Angel Father did teach me how to play, and I show her the way. She cannot look long looks at things, to see how they look not looks alike, because she has no seeing. So she is learning to play comparer by feels.'

In her own Foreword to the *Diary,* Opal wrote,

'And there was Father in those few days when he was home from far lands. Those were wonderful days — his homecoming days. Then he would take me on his knee and ride me on his shoulder and tell me of the animals and birds of the far lands.'

And she tells how she heard of his death,

'The kind woman who taught me and took care of me told me gently that father too had gone to heaven while he was away in the far lands.'

The word 'too' in this account seems to indicate that she had already been parted from her Angel Mother, either by death or in some other way and that she was in the care of this 'kind woman.'

Of her Angel Mother she wrote,

'There were walks in the fields and woods. When on these walks, Mother would tell me to listen to what the flowers and trees and birds were saying. We listened together. And on the way she told me poems and other lovely things, some of which she wrote in the two books and also in others which I had not with me in the lumber camps. On the walks and after we came back, she had me to print what I had seen and what I had heard. After that she told me of different people and their wonderful work on earth. Then she would have me tell again to her what she had told me.'

If this is not a truthful account of what happened it surely indicates a remarkable fantasy of a lonely child, reconstructing in imagination a relationship for which she longed; but much more must be considered before any verdict can be passed on the authenticity of the claim that Opal made about her parentage.

The two notebooks to which she refers are those mentioned by Ellery Sedgwick in his Preface. She wrote of them again when she was listing her few possessions:

'There is my two books that Angel Mother and Angel Father did write in and I do study in every day, and the pictures of mother and père and the pictures of grandmère and grandpère and tante and tante and oncle, and all the others that I do love much everyday; and today there was needs to give the dear picture of père a wash in the brook because last time on yesterday, when I did kiss him, a little piece of jam from my bread and butter got on his dear face that does look so like him.'

Is there any significance in the fact that she gives French titles to all her relatives except her Angel Mother? She does not call her 'mère.' The two aunts and the uncle are not given names. There is no need, from her point of view; she knows who they are and she is not writing for other people who do not.

These two notebooks, Opal said, contained lists of names from history and mythology — the 'different people' who had done 'wonderful work on earth,' — and it was from these lists that she chose the names that she gave to her pets and to the trees in the forest: Aphrodite was the mother-pig; Edward III was 'a fir tree by the singing creek where the willows grow;' Lucian Ovid Horace Virgil was a pet toad and Thomas Chatterton Jupiter Zeus was 'a most dear velvety wood rat.' She confesses that she often spent her time in school studying these books and learning how to spell the names in them when she should have been doing her lessons.

Lord Grey wrote in the Introduction to the *Diary:*

'The mystery of her origin must arouse interest, for the gleams of reminiscence of Angel Father and Angel Mother, slight as they are, give an impression of two people of rare beauty of mind and of feeling.'

No trace has ever been found of the copybooks and photographs, and, apart from the *Diary* itself there is no tangible evidence to support the story of Angel parents. The Whiteley family refused to admit that there was any truth in Opal's claim to be a foster child, and she became estranged from them.

The graphologist who was commissioned to give an opinion on the handwriting of the *Diary* made a thorough study of all the papers that were found amongst Opal's belongings and made the following interesting comment on the apparent disappearance of the notebooks:

'Working on the postulation that Opal is the child of these two persons (Angel Father and Angel Mother) the fact that she was not 'removed' until after the death of Prince Henri would imply that family complications regarding the existence of Opal and her actual parentage, necessitated action of a rather drastic nature. It is evident that every possible trace of Opal's true identity was removed and permanently destroyed during the process of her removal to Oregon, except, by an extraordinary stroke of fate, those two books which evaded the vigilance of those persons responsible for Opal's transit to USA. Those books remained intact in Opal's possession throughout her childhood, but as soon as she received world-wide publicity in the press, and once again the connection with this aristocratic French family was intimated, these books completely disappear. Who would be the most likely person to remove them and destroy them, other than someone specifically instructed to do so, such as a privately or government employed agent or detective? Apparently, the evidence contained in the actual diary is non committal as far as the french family is concerned. Either the anagrams were entirely overlooked or they were not considered worth worrying about, but those books contained a great deal of information of a documentary nature in so far that the handwriting of both parents remained on record — they had to be destroyed at all costs.'

4.

This, then, was the book which more than sixty years ago, astonished and divided the literary world and posed a riddle to which no one seemed able to give an answer. About 15,000 copies of the book were sold in America and a fourth edition was planned, as well as a publication of later parts of the *Diary*. An English edition appeared and sold steadily, but no reprints were made and the rest of the *Diary* was never published.

Slowly Opal was forgotten on both sides of the Atlantic, until in the fifties, her story emerged once more. None of its original interest was lost; the mystery was still there and the *Diary's* strange and haunting quality, which sets it apart from anything that has ever been written by child or adult.

This is how it came about.

When I was a student in the thirties, training to teach young children, a copy of the English edition of the *Diary* was lent to me by the head of the Zoological department. She had been deeply impressed by it and suggested that it would give me an insight into a child's attitude to nature. I read it with great interest; it was to me a moving record of the mind and feelings of a child, something unique and memorable. There are, I suppose, a handful of books in most people's lives whose influence can be felt and traced down the years. This book was such a one for me, and coloured, from then on, my feelings towards wild life and towards children. I read it again and again, to myself, to children and later, as a lecturer myself, to students preparing to teach. On nearly all of them it made a strong impression and set their minds thinking on new lines. Opal was always a very real child to me, and for a quarter of a century she remained a vivid and living personality.

I felt that her diary should be more widely known. Marjorie Flemming, who kept a diary up to her death at the age of eleven, is familiar to many, but few people had heard of Opal Whiteley. In the years that had passed since her *Journal* was published there had been a marked growth of interest in the study of children. I believed that Opal's diary had a valuable contribution to make to such study.

At last, in 1958, I had the opportunity I had always wanted to draw attention to the *Diary*. I was working for the British Broadcasting Corporation, in the Schools Department, and I planned a broadcast about both the children, Marjorie Flemming and Opal.

Before the programme was broadcast I had to find out whether there were any relatives who should be consulted regarding the programme. I made enquiries and was told that Opal had died in hospital ten years before and had left no known relatives. I presumed therefore, that there would be no problems, and the programme went out.

Soon after the broadcast I received a letter from a listener, asking for more information about Opal and where she could get a copy of the *Diary*. I replied, telling her all I knew, which was very little and, in a few days I was surprised to receive a further letter from her, which threw an entirely different light on Opal's story:

'Thank you very much for your advice about obtaining a copy of the *Diary* of Opal Whiteley. Your information about her life convinces me that she is the little person we knew in Hampstead as 'The Little Princess.' So I'll tell you what I know of her:

An Irish friend of mine once met a sad little lady in the

Catholic chapel on the way to Camden Town and took her home to supper. The little lady ate sandwiches in a way that showed she was very hungry and spoke only a little in a soft cultured voice. She was very grateful and of course was asked to come again. Thus began a series of weekly visits which continued over some years. She told my friend that she was a princess of the House of Orleans and that her name was Françoise Marie de Bourbon-Orléans.

My friend made enquiries and learned from the parish priest that she was in fact an American subject who had suffered a head injury during the blitz. Her relationship to the royal house of Orleans was an unfortunate delusion, which caused her to spend her meagre allowance on visits to Sotheby's to purchase books of French history which she couldn't afford.

She talked a lot to my friend, and took her to her room in, I think, South Hill Road, off Haverstock Hill. It was stacked from floor to ceiling with books and magazines: one moved up and down the lanes between books. And there, my friend told me, she saw a thing which shook her. An article in *The Queen* written by 'Princess Françoise de Bourbon-Orléans' — and above it — a photograph of the 'Little Princess' herself! How that came about is still a mystery. For a while, I'm afraid we felt as if the waters were too deep for us to wade in, and the Princess rather worried us.

I met her once only. She wanted to see my baby girl. I felt at home with her at once. I remember a small, rather grubby, graceful and gracious hand, an air of quiet dignity in a small, round person; and brown eyes with an expression at once child-like, appealing, sad and wise. She asked in a gentle way if she might hold the child. I remember handing over the baby rather doubtfully, then felt a pang of envy to see how expertly those little hands soothed it and the quiet voice calmed it. I believe she was a trusted baby-sitter at that time. There is no doubt that she must have found contentment in that sort of work.

All this contributes little to what you already know of Opal

Whiteley, but I'm sure you'll be happy to know that friends of mine took her to their hearts and tables, once a week, during those last years.'

The writer of this astonishing letter can have had no idea of the effect it would have, an effect that was to remain with me for more than forty years. Both she and I were under the impression that Opal was dead and I set off on a long trail, following up the clues the letter had suggested.

My first visit was to the offices of *The Queen* magazine to try to track down the article by 'Princess Françoise de Bourbon-Orléans.' The premises had been bombed during the blitz and many of the records destroyed. I was allowed, however, to go down to the dusty cellars and search among what was left of the old, musty back numbers of the magazine. It seemed a hopeless task and I had almost given up when, suddenly, I came upon an article, published on October 9th 1940. It was called 'The Greatest Hoax in History.'

I took it over to the light by the window to look closer. The subject was Catherine the Great and the author was given as — yes — the Princess Françoise Marie de Bourbon-Orléans. I read the heading:

'The princess is a descendant of the two royal houses of France and is the only child of the late Prince Henri d'Orléans and his cousin, Princess Marie. She has had an adventurous career, following in the footsteps of her father, a famous explorer, and has travelled extensively in India.'

But was this the same person as Opal Whiteley? There was no photograph. Exciting as the discovery was it clearly was not the same article that my correspondent's friend had seen in Opal's room.

I went upstairs to the offices and made enquiries of the editorial staff. No one could throw any light on the matter. All they remembered, after nearly twenty years, was that the author had been 'a strange person, Russian or something,' and that there had been some trouble over payment.

The other clues in my correspondent's letter led nowhere, but at length I heard of someone who was able to tell me the name of the hospital to which Opal had been taken, near St Albans. It was here, I believed, she had died. I wrote to the Medical Superintendent, asking for information. To my astonishment I received the following reply: 'You suggest that you might be able to visit the hospital to discuss Miss Opal Whiteley, and this I think would be the most satisfactory solution. The lady is in fact not dead, but is still a patient here.'

I waited for the day of the interview in a strange tension of feeling. Opal had been a living personality to me for so long I feared disappointment. I felt like someone with his hand on the door of a room he has travelled far to enter, without the courage to open it.

I visited the hospital one day in June and was taken to see the Medical Superintendent. He offered me every assistance and on that and later occasions spent much of his valuable time listening to what I could tell him, a great deal of which was unknown to him. He and the other doctors had treated Opal's claim to royal birth as a delusion. He told me that he considered the unhappy circumstances of her early childhood, however brought about, could have been the cause of her illness.

He sent for Opal.

He spoke of her as 'the Princess,' and when she came into the room he introduced her to me by the same title.

The impact of this first meeting with Opal was something I was not prepared for. She had about her a dignity which I had not expected to find, which made me think at once of Queen Victoria. I saw a small, rather rotund little person, aged about sixty, with greying hair and very large soft brown eyes.

Though shabbily dressed in a badly fitting brown woollen jumper and skirt, she had undoubted graciousness and charm. She held out her small hand to me, a gesture which almost made me feel I should bow over it.

I particularly noticed her hands. They were not the hands of a labourer's child, but unusually small and delicate.

We sat down and she began to talk.

She spoke almost without ceasing for over an hour and showed the same remarkable quality of memory which appears in her diary. In childhood she had memorised the names of the good and great, told to her, as she claimed, by her Angel parents, and now her still-prodigious memory held the names of every crowned and once-crowned head in Europe, with all their cousins and aunts and brothers and nephews. She gave the dates, to the month and the day, of their births and deaths, and many events of their lives and of her own, without faltering for a moment. Prompted by occasional questions she talked without pausing, except when the corners of her mouth drooped in sadness as she spoke of her unfinished writing or stiffened in anger at her imagined wrongs, or when, suddenly, she broke into her sweet and warming smile.

When the interview was over I felt it was I who was being dismissed.

I came away from the hospital with a tangle of confused information and a vivid impression of a fascinating and lively mind. Which of the many stories she had told were true? This strange claim of hers to royal birth, should it be dismissed as a dream of greatness, conceived by a lonely child? What connection was there between her present claim to be a princess of the House of Orléans and the hints in the *Diary* about Angel parents? Could this lonely, highly sensitive and imaginative child have conjured the whole story out of her fertile mind, and in her days and years of study of the Royal House of France had she grown to believe the story she had originally fabricated?

Or was her claim in fact true? Was she, in fact, the great-great-grand daughter of the last King of France? Was it possible that in the early days of the century, troubled days for France and the Royal House, a child, close to the throne, might have been removed, either for political reasons, or for a ransom, and hidden in the rough surroundings of an Oregon lumber camp?

5.

In 1895 the Duke of Orleans had written to A M Buffet: 'La France traverse une crise dont les dangers apparaissent à tous les yeux,' and the following year he was reported to have told a friend of the *Moniteur Universel* to tell his friends to prepare themselves:

'Il ne faut pas que nous soyons surpris par les événements. Je crois que l'année 1896 sera grave. Mes amis peuvent donc compter sur moi comme je compte sur eux.

Ils me trouveront à leur tête et nous serons suivis par tous les hommes de bonne foi que l'expérience du régime républicain en a dégoûtés. Aidons-nous, et le Ciel nous aidera.'

A delegation of the Jeunesse Royaliste de Paris had brought the French flag to him in England on the occasion of his marriage in 1897, and in 1900 exiled Royalists had found their way to York House to persuade him to lead them and return to France.

In these unsettled times anyone of royal blood might have become a centre of unrest and embarrassment, even a girl child of five years. If the child were also illegitimate there would be a different and more personal reason for removing her as far as possible. It has been suggested that it was the-then Premier of France who arranged to have Opal removed, because at that time there was a likelihood of a return of the French aristocracy.

Henry was the pretender, in direct line to the throne, and

the existence of an illegitimate child could have been an embarrassment.

If America seems an unnecessarily distant and unlikely place it can be remembered that Robert, Duke of Chartres, the father of Henry of Orleans, went to the United States with his older brother, the Count of Paris, in 1861, and offered his services to the Federal Government, and that later the Count of Paris visited Canada accompanied by his eldest son, the Duke of Orleans. The American Continent was probably more likely than most places at that time to extend a welcome to exiled royalty. According to recent research on the internet the Boxer Rebellion in 1901 caused a serious threat to Europeans; many were assassinated. America might have seemed the only safe place to hide a child.

A Canadian remembered a visit of members of the French Royal family to his home when he was a boy. He told a reporter that he had sat upon the knees of Henri d'Orléans. His uncle was French and he had formed a friendship with the Comte de Paris in France. After leaving France he had gone to live in Canada, and here the Comte had visited him. His nephew remembered the visit:

'A coach drove up to the house and the comte stepped out, accompanied by another, who was introduced as the Duke of Orleans. The two Frenchman stayed for some time, occupying their time hunting and drinking.'

A note, written under this account in the newspaper reads: 'Probably the son of the Count of Paris — not Henri d'Orléans...'

But whoever these men were, it indicates that there was a link between the French Royal family and North America. Recent research in the internet has thrown up evidence, hitherto unknown, of remarkable links between the Orleans family and Oregon (see chapter 17). It is of particular interest that the boy mentioned in this account eventually moved to Oregon and became City Treasurer of Eastern Oregon. Could he have been 'The man who wears grey neckties and is kind to mice.' Had he been asked to keep an eye on the little Opal?

Since my book was published the evidence of the link between the French Royal family and America has been strengthened. The following facts have come to light:

A cousin of Henry of Orleans led an expedition to Greenland in 1905 and Henry himself, immediately before his death, was planning to visit the United States. This was to have been his next journey. We may keep in mind that Opal, or Françoise, as she wished to be called, would have been a little girl of about five at that time. Was he planning to see her? We can only guess.

This information was given to me by Richard, Lord Acton, nephew of the Hon. Mrs Woodruff, the widow of the Editor of the Catholic newspaper, *The Tablet,* who befriended Opal in England and paid for the storage of her belongings for many years.

Even more interesting is the fact that an earlier member of the Orléans family, before Opal's time, is known to have had a liaison with a well-known singer. There was a child; it was taken away and sent — to Oregon! Was this a coincidence, or was Oregon the place to which these irregular children were always sent?

If the story of Opal's arrival in Oregon were the truth, here was the authentic Fairy Story: the Princess brought up by the Woodcutter.

It is likely that the Whiteleys did not, in fact, know who she was. She may have been brought to them for adoption, without her origin being revealed. Elbert Bede, the Editor of the local paper in Cottage Grove, Oregon, not far from the Whiteley home, spent many years investigating her story. He wrote in *The Sunday Oregonian:*

'My first impression of Opal was that of a vibrant, fluttery, exotic, whimsical person informed strangely beyond her years, eager, deeply earnest, and seriously religious. She later became to me an inexplicable enigma.'

In November 1933, he wrote:

'Opal was an odd child and the only member of the family with an unusually developed love for nature, a personal trait fitting well into the d'Orleans parentage. In so many ways was Opal different from members of the Whiteley family that, without strong supporting evidence for the Whiteley parentage, her story might easily be convincing.'

Sceptics point out the likeness of Opal to her sister. If one were looking for a family to adopt a child it would be natural to seek for one that bore some resemblance to the child, but if one studies the bone structure of the girls' heads, the likeness is less marked.

It seems that members of the Whiteley family, when asked about the truth of Opal's claim to be a foster child, with one exception refused to discuss the matter further after they had once given their opinion. This, Bede said, might be taken as basis for belief that there was more to tell.

Strong evidence in Opal's favour is the story that the mother of d'Orléans, the Duchess of Chartres, accepted Opal and financed her journey to India. This was stated by Elbert Bede in 1933 and also by Mrs Woodruff.

When I saw Opal in hospital she told me that the Duchess of Chartres had sent her to India to find out the circumstances of Henry's death. Amongst her papers I found copies of two letters written by her to the Duchess. She refers to conversations they had had about Prince Henry and to pictures and photographs they had looked at together. She calls him 'the voyager' and the book of which she writes was one she was planning to write about his journeys. It is difficult to believe that she was not referring to an actual meeting.

'Madame of The Rose Garden:

Many thoughts come to me when I wake up in the morning thinking of you and your rose garden. I'm just thrilled to find how you love the forest and it makes you more yet to me beside your being the mother of the voyager, whom as, I hold in reverent esteem because of the honor due to him ... I feel our meeting is like that of long-time friends because there is present that bond of so many common interests your preferences for the wildness of the forest ... Your desire to search about for the rare wild flowers, your love of the companionship of books, your sympathy for horses and dogs, your friendship with birds and your love of flowers. It meant great joy, that at the first meeting with the mother of the voyager, I should find you with so many flowers around you as though they were your friends come to bear you company while the other friends have gone on, and you are not alone.

Referring to Thibetland of which we were speaking while eating cherries the other day I wonder if you have seen On the Eaves of the World by Reginald Farrer.'

The second letter seems to refer to a further visit:

'Madame:

The thought comes to me that for the cover of the book the painting which you showed to me on the wall the one of Monseigneur Henri seated on those steps in the Orient would be excellent for the cover paper with the name of the book.

While continuing my research work at the Bibliothèque Nationale I have noticed a number of photographs appearing at the time of his death, which were not among those we were looking over that day.'

These letters must surely refer to actual meetings of Opal and the Duchess. I find it difficult to believe that it was all no more than a figment of her imagination. One of those who befriended her said that the Duc du Chartres, the Comte de Paris and their uncle, the Prince de Joinville had stayed with her uncle and aunt during the American Civil War. She herself was a friend of Lord Grey. She said she would help Opal to get to France.

Many years later, writing to a priest, Opal tells how she was sent out to India to continue her father's geographical studies and that she had given a promise to the Duchess 'not to enter the cloister but to work for our Lord in the world.'

Opal claimed that one of her grandmothers in the Whiteley family, probably Mrs Whiteley's mother, had told her that she was not a Whiteley and the mystery was further complicated by the fact that this grandmother is known to have given Opal certain heirlooms. None was sent to any other of the grandchildren. Bede wrote:

'Why all the heirlooms should have been sent to one child is a circumstance odd enough to encourage exponents of the foster-parentage claim.'

Opal herself wrote in 1930:

'I was born in Italy thirty-three years ago in February, 1897. My father was Prince Henry of Orleans, the explorer, and my mother was Princess Marie, his cousin. Their secret marriage was strongly disapproved of by both their families but I am so glad they married for love for it has been rather rare in our families.

My earliest recollections are of being held up to touch tree leaves by my grandfather, of listening with mother to all the noises in the garden, of being made to sit still when I wanted to run about all the time; and of being shown the difference between leaves and flowers while father listened to my explaining it all to him. Then he would ride me on his shoulder. Among mother's old letters I have read one where he wrote: "Our Chiquite is very ardent and responsive, so we must teach her to love many things."'

There is clearly some weight of evidence here, but even if it were not so, if the story of Angel Parents were not true, if it were all the fantasy of an unhappy and imaginative child, the importance of the *Diary* is in no way diminished. My purpose in pursuing the story was not to unravel the mystery of Opal's origin, fascinating as it is. I was not concerned about who she really was, nor whether the *Diary* was or was not a true picture of her childhood. The value of the *Diary* is not altered if, in fact, Opal imagined or invented everything she described in it. It is still a record of her thoughts and feelings, a portrait of a sensitive and unusual mind, and therefore of the greatest value as an insight into the nature of children and a reminder to adults, who so quickly forget what it is to be a child, of how intensely children can feel.

In later years, when her mind was failing, Opal was unable to recount memories of her childhood but, in *The Fairyland Around Us,* the book she took to the *Atlantic Monthly,* she gives a haunting memory of an occasion when, as a child, she recalls falling asleep in a church and being carried home by a priest to Angel Mother and Father.

6.

Opal was known as Princesse Françoise de Bourbon-Orléans for over a quarter of a century and was befriended by many well-known people, among them Dean and Mrs Inge, Lady Baden-Powell, Lord and Lady Grey of Fallodon, the Countess of Warwick, Sir Oliver Lodge, the Countess of Iddesleigh and others. She was a guest in their homes and was frequently invited to soirées to meet titled and distinguished people. Amongst her papers I found an invitation to the birthday party of King Feisal of Iraq and notices of her opening fetes and appearing on public occasions under her French title.

An item in the *Evening News* of March 16th 1931, under 'Talk of the Day' read:

'A Bourbon-Orléans Princess in London.

A beautiful young Frenchwoman who is the most direct descendant of Louis Philippe, the last King of France, has just arrived in London.

She is the Princess of Bourbon-Orléans, the daughter of that Prince Henry of Orléans who was born at Ham, near Richmond, after his father, the Duke of Chartres, had fled over to England as a boy with King Louis Philippe.

The Princess is very dark and has lovely brown eyes. She told me that the only country she has not visited recently is France, for she has been a great traveller. When I remarked on her faultless English she told me that she spoke English better than any other language.

Her father was a noted explorer who was killed in Indo-China in 1901. After the death of the Duke of Orleans in 1926 it was her father's younger brother, the Duke of Guise, who became Pretender to the French throne. The Duke of Orleans was well known to Londoners, for he lived most of his life at Twickenham.

An interesting situation will arise when the princess of Bourbon-Orléans decides to act upon her wish to revisit France.

Actually it is only the male Pretender who is banished from French soil; but as the princess is in a more direct line to King Louis Philippe than her uncle, the Duke of Guise, who is the present Pretender, permission may be difficult to obtain. I hear that the League of Nations may be asked to intervene.'

This reference to Opal being in more direct line to Louis Philippe than her uncle is of interest. In her later diaries Opal frequently speaks of an uncle whom she feared and who she believed wished her harm. Could it be that she did, in fact, pose some threat to him, even though, by Salic Law she could never have stood in line to the non-existent throne? The alternative is that her story, as told to the reporter, is a further example of her intense preoccupation with, and research concerning, the French Royal family and their history, and her ability to make people, whose professional job it was to sort fact from fiction, believe her.

The report goes on: 'She has come to London in pursuit of carrying out the last wishes of her father, which were to explore Udaipur, the oldest Kingdom in India. Her immediate duty is to finish writing a book on his discoveries in that fascinating territory. Her father was thirty-three at his death, and she a mere child, but she has remembered his wishes. 'In some ways,' the Princess told me, 'I would prefer not to go to Paris — it will have changed so much since I knew it. But I do want to go to Chartres, the home of my grandfather, Prince Robert, Duc de Chartres.'

The *Evening Standard* of May 9th, published the following:

'Niece of the Pretender to French Throne applies for British Naturalisation.

Princess Françoise Marguerite de Bourbon-Orléans, one of the nearest living descendants of the Kings of France, and niece of the Pretender, has just applied for British naturalisation papers.

The Princess told me today at her home in Buckingham Gate, W, why she wished to become British:

"My father, Prince Henri of Bourbon Orléans, died when I was very young," she said, "and I was 'given' to England in 1903. It was decided that I should pass my life here. Although I have not always lived here since then, I feel very English and I love England, very, very much. So I decided the best thing to do would be to get naturalised.

I am the first member of my family ever to change nationality, but I think it is quite right.

I was born in 1897. On the day I was born my father, who was an explorer and travelled all over the world, left for Abyssinia. He went out to map the region around Harar. While he was out there, he fought for the Abyssinians against the Italians in the campaign of the Summer of 1897. He fought a duel with an Italian during the campaign and the Italian's sword pierced his side.

King Louis Philippe, the last of the Bourbon Kings, was my great-great-grandfather. There he is." She showed me an old colour-print.

"I am in the direct line of descent. My uncle, the Duc de Guise, is the head of the family today. I am also related to King Charles X of France.

I love my France very much. I have not been there for years. I can only go for a visit, as the law at present forbids me to live there. Now that I am to be English, I think I shall be able to go back.'

A number of geographical, botanical and historical societies admitted Opal to membership under her royal title. All expressed themselves honoured to accept her. The societies concerned were:

Société Archéological de Bordeaux
Société Géologique de Bretagne
Société Géologique de France
Société Préhistorique Française
Société de Géographie d'Alger
Société Botanique de France.

Her Journey to, and residence in India is of particular interest. She lived there for ten months during 1924 and 1925, under the name of Madame Dorlay. She was a guest in the Palace of the Maharana and, according to Opal herself, was privileged to witness ceremonies that no white woman had ever seen before.

The Times, which is in the habit of checking its facts, was of the opinion that she was related to the Indian Prince, for it printed on the Society page the information, 'Miss Opal Whiteley, grand-daughter of the Maharana of Udaipur, has left London for India.'

An American woman travelling in India brought back the story that she had seen Opal driving in an open carriage down the streets of Allahabad, during a ceremonial procession, the purpose of which was to proclaim her as a Hindu Princess. The carriage was drawn by a number of white horses, and royal outriders cleared the way in front of her. The American woman had known Opal and was sure it was she.

The *Morning Oregonian* of September 1933 reporting the story, said: 'Discreetly the traveller made enquiry and learned that the haughty woman in the carriage, escorted by the house cavalry of His Royal Highness the Maharana of Udaipur, was a dweller in the palace and a near relation of the Maharana.'

Robert Nassif Lindsey, composer and author of the Musical *Opal* often visited 'the princess' at Napsbury. On one occasion he questioned her about her relationship to the Maharana:

'Did he accept you as a grand-daughter?'

Her reply was, 'No, he *treated* me like a grand-daughter.'

Her real grandfather, she said, was Grand Duke Ferdinand of Florence.

The American woman who had been so amazed at the brilliant apparition in the streets of Udaipur recalled other odd things she had heard — that Opal Whiteley had left the United States very secretly, travelling not with an ordinary passport, but with the aid of a confidential document signed by an American Secretary of State and Sir Edward Grey of England for the British Foreign Office. And eventually the tale got about that the strange gifted child and woman, Opal Whiteley, was actually the daughter of a scion of the noble French line of Orleans and Artois, of royal blood, and of his wife, a daughter of the Maharana of Udaipur. Dr Rushford Williams, foreign minister for his Highness the Maharajah of Patiala, also a native state of Rajputana, told this writer two years ago that a young American woman was actually residing at the Udaipur royal palace, evidently a member of the royal family.

Ellery Sedgwick was not satisfied with the truth of this report and, since it concerned two of the greatest Indian Princes and claimed that they had been Opal's hosts, he wrote to both their courts for confirmation.

'In due time,' he wrote in *The Happy Profession,* 'two letters returned, emblazoned with regal crests, each informing me the writer's royal master bade the secretary reply that it had been his high privilege to entertain HRH Mlle Françoise de Bourbon-Orléans, and that a series of fetes had been given to do her honour.' A letter, dated 21st October 1929 from the Private Secretary to Shreeman Maharaj Kumar Sahib Bahadur, to Mademoiselle D'Orléans, reads:

'I am directed by Shreeman Maharaj Kumar Sahib Bahadur to inform you that Mr Ellery Sedgwick, Editor of the *Atlantic Monthly,* Boston, Massachusetts, USA, has been informed that you were in Udaipur from about September, 1924, to about June, 1925, and that you extensively moved about in the State to different places.'

Another letter reads:

'His Highness the Maharana of Udaipur requests me to say that it will give him much pleasure if you will come to tea on the Jagmandir Island at 4.45 pm. on 8th January 1925, to have the honour of meeting Their Royal Highnesses Prince and Princess Arthur of Connaught.'

Yet another letter, from H R Pritchard, Mewar residency, Udaipur, 10th September 1924, contains the following:

'The Durbar are very interested to hear of the reason of your visit to Udaipur, and in view of the fact that you wish to collect material for the compilation of a history of Mewar they trust that you will consider yourself a guest of the State during your stay at Udaipur.

Orders have been given for your reception in the State Guest House from tomorrow.'

It is impossible to discount this information and one can only assume that Opal held some sort of privileged position at the Maharana's court.

When he died she wrote to *The Times*,

'May I also add my tribute of respect and affection to the memory of that grand Seigneur of India, HH The Maharana of Udaipur, who has just left us, his friends, lonelier for his passing but richer in life's experience with the remembrance of his perfect courtesy. To have known him was an education in itself and I feel one of the few great privileges of a life time. To his never-failing consideration and exquisite gentleness while I was residing in his state, I owe a debt which it seems to me I never can repay. He was not a Christian but he had many ways of the Christian gentleman and sometimes made me think of St Paul.

It was during 1924 and 1925 that I lived for ten months in his kingdom, that stronghold of orthodoxy and likewise of loyalty to the British Raj. I went there incognito to make notes of the legends, customs, festivals, archaeology and natural history for a book on Udaipur; and through my many trials he was steadfastly loyal and helpful to me in a hundred different ways. And he seemed to have a deep appreciation of the task I had undertaken and was never too busy to stop from other things to talk to me about some detail of it. If I was sad he would send me a beautiful pomegranate, or milk from his own cow; or play the fountains so that I could hear the music of their water; or show me through his window the panorama of the exquisite Pichola lake; or talk to me about the flight of birds, or the paths of the stars, or the Upanishads. And when the elephant I was on pranced when we were after panther he got down and had me climb on his own horse. I think he thought of me as a little child and sometimes he would call me "the little sister of the birds and flowers." He felt my being in his state was a great responsibility and when there were perilous days in my work the Maharana Sahib put me in charge of the one man he trusted most completely in all his kingdom.

Though I loved animals too much to shoot them, Maharana Sahib very often took me on "Shikar" with him that I might see the panorama of animal life, and during the long period of waiting in the shooting box he would work on his state papers while I wrote down notes for my book on Udaipur. Sometimes while we waited for a tiger in a machan, high up in a tree to which he had climbed at 76, he would cut wings from tree-leaves and send them to fly out like birds to please the small boy and me who were on either side of him.

He was equally reverent and simple on that great occasion when he was in his "divine office" as High Priest and mediator between God and his people on "the Holy Night of Mahadev" in February. I have been told I am the only European who was ever allowed to see this ceremony. I shall never forget it. His people were about him as a shepherd and with all his austerity and remoteness that night because of his sacerdotal role, he was omnipresent and the most gentle among them. It was always a comfort to me to see how his people tried to emulate his courtesy. So they made me feel that Udaipur was for a little time my home.'

7.

It was Opal's account of this journey to India that appeared in a series of articles in *The Queen* at the end of 1929 and the beginning of 1930, and which had so surprised my correspondent's friend in Hampstead.

They were illustrated by a number of remarkable photographs, taken by her, both of the country and of ceremonies which she claimed she had been privileged to witness, but which no other European woman had seen before. The heading reads:

'Princess Françoise Marie de Bourbon-Orléans Begins The Story of Unknown India,' and under a photograph of Opal herself is the caption: 'Princess Françoise de Bourbon-Orléans is the daughter of the explorer, Prince Henri d'Orléans.'

The first article begins:

'From the first week of September, 1924, to the end of June, 1925, while en route to Dar-Lac, my father's last field of exploration, I passed ten months in that surpassingly beautiful Country of the Sun-King, the last stronghold of old India yet under the rule of an ancient etiquette and millenium-old traditions.

I arrived at Chitor at night and could only see as a ghostly outline this old fortress deserted for three hundred years, and rising now as a phantom ship out of the desert. I had heard that every stone of Chitor speaks, so I went to investigate next morning — and found that this was true. There is a melancholy aspect in its fallen palaces, suspended balconies and hanging domes — all of a wondrous honeycomb golden-brown colour. I muse that in this very place are hidden and lost trails where trod the feet of the Lotus Queens and those other high-hearted Rajput women when they went to the sacrifice. For all India swears by the "three-and-a-half-sacks of Chitor." Each is haunted with the memory of those devoted women who went with iron wills to embrace death through the flames rather than to be dishonoured by the approaching enemy. And when the conquerors entered the capital triumphant, their triumph was quickly turned to gall, for they found neither maidens nor wives. Alone, their ashes kept midnight watch. Yes — even after six hundred years the stones of Chitor cry aloud.' We recognise the voice of the little Opal, confiding to her *Diary* her intense feelings about Peter Paul Rubens and Michael Angelo Sanzio Raphael, still feeling as intensely, and still romantic.

She intended to expand the articles into a book, to be called *The Sun King and his Kingdom in Unknown India.* Both her English and her American publishers were actively interested in publishing it. The Superintendent of Napsbury Hospital offered her all the facilities and help she wanted but, in spite of all the encouragement she received, she never completed the book.

A letter appeared in the *Observer* Weekend Review for 16th September 1962, signed C G Chenivix Trench:

'I am in a position to throw light on the mystery, having seen a great deal of Opal Whiteley in the years 1922-1927 when I was in the ICS (Indian Civil Service) and "lent" i.e. forced upon His Highness the Maharana of Udaipur, whose muddle-headedness had reduced his State to near-anarchy. He was a most formidable old man.

Opal turned up one day in his capital, the beauty spot of India, with nothing but the clothes she was wearing. She was at once lodged in a marble pavilion in the palace garden and given a bodyguard of six aboriginal Bheels. That in itself was significant, for his Highness's anti-British sentiments were notorious. Opal then called herself, indifferently, Mlle D'Orle, Mlle Ecrivain or Miss Whiteley.

She was a small, dark woman of about thirty and might have passed for a Eurasian. Her oval face was childish but her expression "rusée."

My wife fitted her out with clothes and she was constantly in and out of our house. The professed object of her visit was to write a history of the Rajputs but nothing came of that, and what puzzled my wife and myself was her nationality and background. Her English was infantile and she spoke vile French, but her famous diary, which she brought with her was undoubtedly genuine. Lord Grey of Fallodon had written an enthusiastic preface to it in which, incidentally, he invokes blessings on a character who figures in it, 'The man who wears grey neck-ties and is kind to mice.'

After some months in Udaipur she showed my wife an enormous framed and signed photograph of the Duke of Orleans. She claimed him as her father and I saw, and still see no reason to doubt her statement.'

The possibility that she might be the grand-daughter of an Indian Prince found some confirmation in a photograph printed in the *Sunday Oregonian* for May 13th 1934. This was of the Maharana of Udaipur, said by *The Times* to be her grandfather. There is a strong resemblance between him and Opal, and it seems that he had three daughters, one of whom could possibly have been her mother. In addition, Elbert Bede reports that, at the time of the death of Henry of Orleans, there was a story current of an unhappy love affair in India.

The Internet gives information of a book, written in French under an assumed name and never translated, that tells of Henri's time in Asia. It said that he 'had a "bedding companion" who called herself a princess.'

A doctor, living in Dorset, England, an Indian herself, saw a photograph of Opal as a young girl and exclaimed, 'She is exactly like my mother!' and while my earlier book was in production a letter was found, dated Udaipur, Sept. 1925, sending greetings to Opal in Bombay, calling her 'my dear daughter Sahebji' and signed 'Payari Bai.'

Miss Elna Merrick of Homer, New York, knew Opal in America. She wrote, 'She was such a charming young person, always beautifully groomed — exquisite. We could always believe her story of Indian heritage — her hands, eyes, the lustre of her hair and the slight colour of her skin — all bore that out.' But was she speaking of the India of the Orient or of American Indian?

She went on, 'She had an amazing way of getting influential people interested in her. She insisted that if she could get to Europe, she could prove her identity, but there was the question of a passport. Just how she managed it I never knew, but she got the passport through the Hon. Charles Evans Hughes who was at that time our Secretary of State. Mr Hughes was not an easily persuaded man, so she must have presented a real case.'

This correspondent also told me that Opal said that she had kept the diary in a box under her bed until the younger Whiteley children had torn it up to annoy her — then she hid it in the woods.

Although Opal was apparently received into the household of the Maharana, possibly as a member of his family, it has never been established that she was related to him and the question of who her mother was has never been settled. The Whiteley family always maintained that she was the daughter of Mrs Whiteley, but if they had been paid to bring her up and to conceal her true identity it would be most unlikely that they would say anything else, and on the question of her likeness to her sister Pearl it would be reasonable to believe, if she were to be 'fostered incognito' that a family would be chosen that she resembled.

In the Foreword to the *Diary* Opal herself said that her

mother had been drowned, but later on she changed the story, and when I saw her in hospital she told me that this was not in fact so. The caption to the article in *The Queen* said that her mother was a cousin of Prince Henry, Princess Marie and this is what Opal herself wrote in 1930. Later on, she claimed for her mother an Archduchess of Austria, a daughter of Alice of Toscana.

I was given some interesting information which relates to the suggestion that she could be related to the Toscanas by the Hon. Mrs Woodruff, who befriended her over a long period and knew her well. During the Spanish civil war Mrs Woodruff was working as a nurse in the Pamplona Military Hospital. It happened that a member of the Toscana family was there at the same time. On seeing her for the first time Mrs Woodruff told me she was immediately struck by her resemblance to Opal. 'When she walked into the room,' she told me, 'my husband and I both said "Françoise!"'

Photographs of the Bourbon-Orléans family show a surprising likeness to Opal. In one of these, the present Pretender and his father, the Comte de Paris, look very unlike one another, while the likeness between the Pretender and Opal is quite striking. Ellery Sedgwick told how a correspondent of his received a photograph claimed to be of Opal's grandfather, the Duke of Chartres. He wrote: 'The likeness of the so-called grandfather to Opal herself was in my estimation clear and striking. In fact it has done much to support my belief in Opal's mysterious origin.'

Constant Huntington, the Chairman of Putnam, wrote to Lady Warwick in July 1931, 'My wife finds in her a great resemblance to portraits of the Empress Charlotte of Mexico.' — the Empress Charlotte was a granddaughter of King Louis Philippe — 'and she finds in memoirs of the family descriptions of many women of Françoise's type.'

Members of the French Royal Family repudiated Opal's claim and called her an imposter. One of them wrote:

'I find it better to tell you very frankly that the *soit-disant* P'sse Françoise de Bourbon Orléans has nothing whatever to do with our family,' but one of the reasons given for this assurance cannot be taken seriously. The letter goes on:

'She met my Uncle, P'ce Henri, during his travel to India,' but as Prince Henry died in 1901, when Opal was four or five, and as she did not go to India until 1924 this would have been impossible.

Huntington repeatedly urged Opal to establish her identity by some kind of acceptable proof. He went so far as to make an appointment for her with a lawyer of the Society of Authors. Opal did not keep the appointment and refused to press her claim in face of the opposition she met. The widow of the Bishop of London, Mrs Creighton, wrote to Constant Huntington in November 1929, 'That she believes herself to be Prince Henri's legitimate daughter I have no doubt, but the Orléans family seem to be most mysterious and much given to family disputes, and I should think the truth might be difficult to get at.

She has become very sensitive as to the enquiries that have been made by some people who doubt her word, and this one can readily understand. Those who have not seen her, say at once that she must be a mere adventuress, but I do not think that one can see her and talk with her and believe that.'

Most people who knew her well believed firmly that she was not a conscious imposter, even if they had doubts about her claims. Huntington, writing to Ruth Putnam in February 1920, said,

'Thank you for your letter about our little 'Princess.' She is a touching creature and no one who sees much of her can possibly dismiss her as nothing but a fraud. Such people as Lord Grey of Fallodon, Mrs Creighton, Lady Pinhey and many others know her well and feel a great kindness for her. She may not know the truth of her own story herself.'

A letter from Constant Huntington in December 1929 suggests a reason for her unwillingness to press her claims:

'I am sure she is sincere in her own belief and genuinely sensitive and nice-minded, but her shrinking from exploitation has the effect of preventing her from giving us conclusive proof and the possibility remains in one's mind that the whole thing may be some extraordinary delusion.'

He received this reply from a friend of the French Royal Family:

'I quite feel with you that there may be more in the little lady than just a delusion, but I don't feel I can do any more as obviously the family don't like her. (It may be for one reason or another!)'

Huntington, writing to Lord Grey in December 1929, reaffirms his belief in her integrity:

'About her Orleans connection I feel sure that there is some mystery and possibly irregularity. I feel confident that it is not an invention or delusion, however. One can easily imagine a perfectly simple explanation of Opal's reticence and the lack of sympathy among members of the family.' In plain words, that she was illegitimate and therefore an embarrassment to them.

One piece of evidence came to light recently, which could be significant. This is a letter from an American Attorney at Law, stating that Mrs Whiteley had told him that Opal was adopted. He was G Evert Baker, one-time president of the Christian Endeavor for Oregon. If he is correct in his memory — he stated that he had met Mrs Whiteley, with Opal — this is perhaps the one missing fact that is needed. We can only believe in his accuracy. He is not mentioned by Elbert Bede in his book, *The Fabulous Opal Whiteley*. It might appear that the omission was deliberate.

He wrote to Opal on June 20, 1920:

'You will recall our first meeting at the District Convention held at Cottage Grove in April 1911. It was my first Convention after I was elected President of the Oregon Christian

Endeavor Union.

That Sunday afternoon I was speaking on God's Great Out-of-Doors ... While thus speaking, I noticed a dark-haired girl with big-round eyes in the center of the church.

After the meeting adjourned you and the lady with you came to the rear of the Church ... You informed me concerning what you had been doing and the interest you had taken in out-of-door life, whereupon I stated that you had the background for a wonderful work among the children ... We had quite a long talk, and you asked me if you could have the little poem that I gave that afternoon, which I promised to send you after reaching home, and which I did send.

After we had talked some little time, you went to one side with some of the other girls and the lady that was with you that afternoon continued to talk with me, and at that time advised me that you were an orphan child ...

On arriving home, I spoke to Mrs Baker, concerning the little girl I met and also told her what the lady with you told me, and as I remember now, it was Mrs Whiteley herself. Mrs Baker remembered very clearly that I spoke of you as being an orphan child.

In a few days I copied the little poem and mailed it to you, and immediately thereafter received a letter from Mrs Whiteley thanking me again for doing so much for you,and said it was very good of me to take so much of my time, as she knew I was a busy man, and give it to an homeless child.'

There is also a quote from the *Atlantic Monthly* papers stating that Mrs Whiteley told several people that Opal and another were not her children. That was discounted because of Mrs Whiteley's mental problems.

8.

On the last occasion on which I saw Opal, eighteen months before her death, she was in an advanced state of senility. She was barely able to communicate at all, but two of the questions we asked her she answered without any hesitation. They were:

'What is your name?'

'Françoise!'

'Who was your father?'

'Henry of Orleans.'

She said no more and relapsed into the silence of her failing powers. We were left with the question, when one is senile does one tell the truth, or does one still live with a fantasy?

As far as the present book is concerned, however, the question of who Opal was is not of primary importance, although one is inevitably drawn into it by the very nature of the problem of whether or not the diary is genuine. Nevertheless, if one believes the diary to be authentic — and Ellery Sedgwick wrote to me — 'I have no doubt that the original diary of Opal Whiteley was entirely genuine. I took endless pains to establish her story' — there are many things that are difficult to explain. Much of the *Diary* is hard to accept as the work of a child brought up in the surroundings of a lumber camp, with the limited education that Opal evidently had.

If she were truly the child of an Oregon lumberman, how was she able to draw on the wealth of knowledge which is evident in the *Diary?* In particular, how can one account for her knowledge of the French language, which she uses with such ease?

'The leaves did sing. The grasses talked in whispers all along the way. I have thinks they were saying, "Petite Françoise, l'été approche — l'été approche!"

And all the voices that did speak — they were grey tones: "Petite Françoise. C'est jour gris!"

'While I did listen I did have hearings of the talkings of the wind and petite plants just having begins to grow out of the earth. The wind did say, "Je viens — je viens." The plants did answer make, "Nous entendons — nous entendons!" So they did speak. Then the wind did say, "Le Printemps viendra bientôt!" And the plants did answer make, "Nous fleurions bientôt."

When we were come to the meeting of the roads, we went the way of the road that goes to the upper camps. We made no stops until we were come to where a long time ago the road had a longing to go across the rivière, and some men that had understanding made it a bridge to go across it. When we were come to the bridge, we made a stop and I did sing to the rivière a song. I sang it the Chant de Seine, de Havre, et Essone et Nonette et Roullon et Iron et Darnetal et Ourcq et Rille et Loing et Eure et Audelle et Nonette et Sarc. I sang it as Angel Father did teach me to, and as he has wrote it in the book.'

This list is, to all appearances, an innocent recital of a random collection of French rivers, and as such it appeared in *The Journal* and the *Diary* and passed without comment, until one day a reader examined it and certain other lists of flowers and birds which appear in the *Diary* and made the remarkable discovery: that if one takes the first letter of each of these rivers, after Seine, it will be found that they spell the name Henri d'Orléans.

Another list, this time of birds, gives the name of Prince Henry's father, Robert d'Orléans, whom Opal called her grandfather:

'I did sing to Brave Horatius the bird song of grandpère of roitelet and ortolan and bruant and étourneau and rossignol and tourterelle and durbec and orfraie and roussette and loriot and nonnette and sarcelle and draine and epeiche and cygne and hirondelle and aigle and ramier and tarin and rousserolle and émerillon and sittelle.'

Other lists give the names Marie and Marguerite, whom she called her aunts; Françoise Marie d'Orléans, Prince Henry's mother and Robert François Louis Philippe Ferdinand Marie d'Orléans, whom she called uncle, and also the dates of their birthdays.

The discovery was revealed to Ellery Sedgwick who, for a time, refrained from telling Opal herself what had come to light. His reason for withholding the information was that she was still engaged in piecing together the rest of the *Diary* and he felt that, if she were to have an inkling of the secret that was being unfolded, any further discoveries would have less value.

It seems that the Bourbon family enjoyed acrostics and anagrams and rhymes of this kind — Opal herself said 'Our family used anagrams. They used them all the time. They were recited, not sung.' And the possible conclusion is that Opal learned these strings of names in childhood without realizing what they signified. What adds some weight to the evidence is the fact that there are mistakes in the lists; sometimes a name is omitted which breaks the sequence, or another substituted. This seems like the natural inaccuracy of a child. If the lists were added later to the *Diary* with the intention of proving Opal's claim, as some critics have suggested, it seems reasonable to think that such mistakes would not have been allowed to pass:

'More songs Angel Father did teach me to sing of birds of oncle, of roitelet, ortolan, bruant, épervier, rousserolle, tourterelle, farlouse, ramier, aigle, nonnette, chardonneret, orfraie, ibis, rossignol, loriot, ortolan, ibis, sansonnet, pinson, hirondelle, ibis, lanier, ibis, pic, pivoine, épeiche, faisan, étourneau, roitelet, draine, ibis, nonnette, aigle, niverolle, durbec, aigle, roitelet, ibis, étourneau, draine, ortolan, roitelet, ibis, étourneau, draine, ortolan, roitelet, loriot, émerillon, aigle, niverolle, sarcelle.

The first letters of each name spell: ROBERT FRANCOIR LOIS PHILIPPE FERDINAND ARIE DORLEANS. R has been substituted for S at the end of Francois, U has been omitted from Louis and the initial M from Marie.

Opal herself was apparently puzzled by the French words which appeared in her diary. In a letter to Mr Whiteley, written in April 1920, at the time the *Journal* was appearing in the *Atlantic Monthly,* she asks if he can give her an explanation. The letter throws light on their relationship and on the effect the publication of the *Journal* had on the Whiteley family:

'You ask me what in the world is the matter with me? Nothing is. I am not having vagaries of mind. And as to what you say about who has been telling me all such stuff. No one has. You ask if I can't change that or have I sold it. Sold or unsold, it couldn't be changed — it's the diary as it is, just as I printed it when I was a very little girl. As the diary goes on there are many things in it which my own mother and own father taught me.

You said for me to write to tell you of all my troubles. It was kind for you to say that. It was the first time you have ever said it in my life. I was glad you wrote it in this letter. One time when I was in the fourth grade at Taylor's Camp you helped me with an arithmetic problem. It made me very glad. I have always remembered it. I wanted you to know.

You said that my diary is causing you a lot of trouble. I am sorry and I regret the annoyance the reporters have caused you. But really the trouble isn't yours — it is mine, because I would like so much to know more about my own father and mother. I want so very much to have again the two books they wrote in. Do you have any idea where my two books are? They were taken while we were at George Taylor and Son's Camp at Vaughan's Spur.

Can you tell me anything about the French in my diary?

I do not know French now and haven't for years. I never knew I knew it until we came across French words in my diary. They are there and they are spelled correctly. What about them? You said for me to tell you my troubles. That is one of them — What about the French in my diary?

Please do write soon and do answer my questions. I had hoped so very much that you would tell me something about my own mother and father. I do so want to know more about them. Won't you tell me what you know?'

Opal refers to herself throughout the *Diary* as Françoise:

'All along the way I kept hearing voices. Little leaves were whispering, "Come petite Françoise."

The wind comes creeping in under the door. It call, "Come, come, petite Françoise, come." It calls to me to come go explores. It does pipe the gentle song the forest sings on grey days. I hear all the voices calling me. I listen — but I cannot go.'

Certain constructions sound strange and awkward in her writing. Was this because she was struggling to write in English and, though bilingual, still thinking in French?

'The man of the long step. The most high stump.

I have wonders where is Brave Horatius. He comes not at my calling. Two days he is now gone. For him I go on searches.

The sounds that were in time of Summer are not now.

The stars were not and dark was before we were come home. But the man that wears grey neckties and is kind to mice, he did have knows of the way of the road by night.

I had thinks some little life was much hurt and did have needs of my help.'

I was told by an english friend that the construction Opal uses in her writing is similar to that used by her english son, brought up in France, struggling to speak and write in english, particularly the use of such phrases as 'I did have' instead of 'I had,' and I have noticed similar construction in the speech of young children learning to speak.

Opal said that there were no books in the Whiteley home beyond 'a cook book, a doctor book and an almanac.' How was it, then, that she was familiar with Titian's picture, *L'homme au gant?* The original of this is in the Louvre. Was it possible that she saw it there as a young child?

'Jenny Strong has little ruffles around the neck of that dress, like the ruffles that was around the neck of the man with the glove when Titian made his picture.'

Why, in her imaginative game on the kitchen floor, did she choose to call the forest through which she was pretending to walk, the forêt de Chantilly. Chantilly was the home of the Princes de Condé and, after the Revolution, of the Duc d'Aumale, a Prince of the House of Orléans. Nonette, Lounette and Aunette are small streams in the neighbourhood. This seems obscure knowledge to be familiar to a child in a lumber camp in the far west of America.

'Raindrops were beginning to come down from the sky. Their coming was in a gentle way. I had longs to be out with them.

While I did watch the raindrops I had longs to go to the forêt de Chantilly and adown by Nonette. I did have thinks more about it. I took some of the wood out of the wood-box. I stood it up for trees. I called them all forêt de Chantilly. We went a walk between them — Lucian Horace Ovid Virgil (a pet toad) and I did. Then I took a dipper full of water and let it pour in little pours a rivière on the kitchen floor. That was for Nonette. Then all of us went a walk by Nonette. We went in little steps to make the time go longer. I took some more water and the dipper and I made it go a little rivière to join Nonette. Then we went a little walk by Lounette. And more I did pour in little pours to join Nonette. That was for Aunette.

After we did have walks all in between the forêt de Chantilly, and I took more sticks from the wood-box back of the stove and I made another forêt. Then we went walking in the forêt d'Ermenonville. When we were come back from the walk, I made some lions out of cheese. Two I made. I made them to put in the forêt de Chantilly at the begins of the route du Connétable.'

Opal had not left America when the *Diary* was published, yet here she shows a surprisingly detailed knowledge of the map of this part of France. In a later part of the *Diary,* which was never published, she described in detail a part of France closely connected with the French Royal family, including the numbers of a street in Paris and of a house in which she claims she lived as a child. On the back of the sheets which comprise this part of the diary are some sketches. One of these, of a building, has been identified. Even more strange is the fact that the sketches appear to have been made from the windows of the house itself, and their accuracy was confirmed by an American woman who had once lived in France.

9.

If Opal were the child of the Whiteleys it is difficult to explain her familiarity with the ritual of the Roman Catholic church. She is careful to see that all her pets are baptised and takes them to Cathedral Service in the woods, where she sings the Angelus, the Sanctus, Sanctus, Sanctus and the Ave Maria to them. The Whiteleys were Protestant if they were anything. Opal herself said they were atheists and never went to church.

She wrote in her diary:

'Today I did go in quick steps to the tree I have planted for Louis Philippe roi de France, for this is the day of his borning in 1773. I did have prayers. Then I did light my little candle. Seventy six big candles Angel Father did so light for him, but so I cannot do, for only one little candle I have. It did burn in a bright way. Then I did sing, "Deo Gratias." I so did sing for the borning day of Louis Philippe, roi de France. Then I did sing "Sanctus, sanctus, sanctus, Dominus Deus."'

This would seem to come from the heart, from a familiarity with the Catholic ritual such as could only be experienced by someone who had grown up, in childhood, in such an atmosphere. It seems part of the air she breathes and utterly natural to her. One feels it could never have been written by a Protestant child. If the idea of foster parents were an illusion, how was so young a child able to draw on a culture wholly foreign to her actual background?

She shows in the *Diary* an extensive knowledge of the lives

Opal Whiteley claimed to be the daughter of Prince Henry of Orleans, the Pretender to the throne of France.

Opal wrote her diary on any scraps of paper she could find. The frame surrounding her writing is characteristic of the work of an insecure child.

She took 19 months to piece together the torn fragments of her diary. *Photo: Bachrach.*

The writing shows Opal's developing hand.

The Whiteley family, said to be Opal's adoptive parents, were Oregon lumber people.

The source of it all: the Oregon woodland that inspired a child's communion with nature.

The two Whiteley sisters. On the right is the 'original' Opal before the alleged substitution with Françoise.

Did Opal look like her supposed sister? Many have explored the possibilities. Here she is on the left.

The Opal countryside. The ‘singing creek’ and ‘blue hills’ beyond.

Overcrowded? Opal’s school room (she is in the right hand row, third seat from front) was unlikely to have provided a rich education. She was very small, perhaps older than she claimed to have been when she wrote the diary.

Prince Henri, Opal's 'Angel Father' died when she was very young. The Bourbon-Orleans family always disclaimed her french parentage.

Here is Opal age 16 (on left) with her alleged sister. A resemblance?

The older Opal became, the more her writing lost its child-like spontaneity. A picture from her book *The Fairyland Around Us*.

Opal tried to get into films. Not a success!

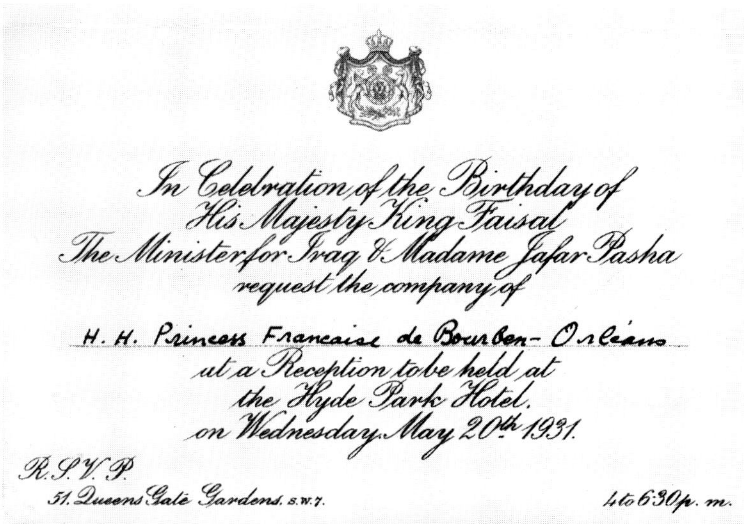

In Celebration of the Birthday of
His Majesty King Faisal
The Minister for Iraq & Madame Jafar Pasha
request the company of

H. H. Princess Francaise de Bourbon-Orléans

at a Reception to be held at
the Hyde Park Hotel.
on Wednesday May 20th 1931.

R.S.V.P.
51. Queens Gate Gardens. S.W.7.

4 to 6.30 p. m.

Opal was accepted as royalty.

Viscount Grey of Fallodon, a man of learning and scholarship, was unlikely to have got Opal wrong.

American interest in Opal is much alive. Robert Nassif Lindsey's musical proves it!

Opal in her 50's at Napsbury Hospital.

Why did the distinguised attend Opal's funeral at Highgate Cemetery?

and deeds of the great of many ages, calling her pets after them and noting their birthdays and their 'going-away' days. It is difficult to reconcile such knowledge with the simple schooling and limited background of a lumber camp, even though she is remembered as an outstanding child.

At school she was known to be dreamy and studious. One of her teachers called her the most intellectual child in the school; she passed through two grades in one year. Another teacher recognized that she was not like other children, but believed her to be honest and sincere. The Superintendent of one of the schools she attended described her as the type of student one never forgets.

'At school,' he wrote, 'she brought life to all she did and showed intense interest in whatever she was doing. It is easy to be deceived in regard to her mental development, since she was modest and retiring as well as being small, but she showed her ability in her capacity for work and the way in which she analysed any problem or subject. Her enthusiasm for botany, zoology and geology was outstanding and she made and classified collections of hundreds of specimens.'

A correspondent who knew her as a child wrote, 'Opal was brilliant and a genius, but very dreamy. She was an idealist, and had a great desire for recognition. From earliest childhood she was interested in nature and at one time had all the neighbor children picking up caterpillars for her, until she had a whole barrel full. The other children thought she was odd. Her younger sister, Pearl, was more friendly and outgoing, while Opal was more aloof.

She was not as well accepted by her peers and elders as the rest of the family was, but she could relate to the younger children and this she did. She seemed to rather be by herself most of the time.'

At University she was known to be different. Inez Fortt, one time librarian in the University, wrote, 'She was a strange and lonely girl, one of five children. Opal was certainly different from the others. She lived a life apart, enveloped in a fantasy world populated by little companions of the woods.'

There is no doubt that she had remarkable ability. All those with whom she came in contact speak of the scope of her mental capacity, and it is difficult to believe, in the face of such evidence, that her origin could have been commonplace.

The Oregonian wrote of her in March 1918, two years before the appearance of the *Diary:* 'When Opal was small, she spent much time in the fields and woods observing the birds, flowers and butterflies and keeping notebooks of her observations. "When I was a child I was always wanting to know how and why," she said. "I asked questions constantly and when the grown-ups couldn't tell me, I sought my answers in nature, turning last of all to books."

She always had a lot of pets of all kinds: turtles, caterpillars, birds, bunnies, squirrels, cats, lizards, frogs and even a pet skunk and a deer.'

There are photographs of the deer and the skunk in *The Fairyland Around Us.* The article in the *Oregonian* goes on: 'She named her pets after characters in history and opera. A pet lizard was honoured with Rigoletto. She named twelve caterpillars after Jacob's twelve sons.

In her work with the children of the lumber camps one of the most beautiful ideas for them was the cathedral in the woods where she met with the children Sundays and sometimes in the evening for the twilight hour.'

From her earliest childhood Opal had learned to be a close observer of nature:

'After I did dish-towel all the dishes that we did use in the breakfast meal, the mamma did send me to get barks for the warming stove. While I was getting barks I did stop to screwtineyes the plump wiggles that were in and under all the barks. Those plump wiggles will grow and change.

They will grow and change into beetles. I have seen them do so. I have taken them from the bark and they did so grow into beetles — after some long time. In the nursery I kept them while they did so change.'

Here is the true naturalist. She knew because she had seen for herself.

'As I did go on, I did have sees there were earthworms on the window-panes over the young cabbage-plants. The grown-ups say the earthworms rained down. They are mistaken. Those earthworms crawled up. I've watched them do it.

I made a stop by a hazel bush. I did stop to watch a caterpillar making his cradle. He did not move about while he made it. He did roll himself up in a leaf. That almost hid him. He did weave white silk about him. The silk a caterpillar makes its cradle from does come from its mouth. I have seen it so. But not so have I seen come the silk the spider does make its web of. This silk does come from the back part of the back of the spider.'

It has been suggested that much of her knowledge, particularly of nature, was given to her by an uncle, a brother of Mrs Whiteley. Opal wrote, in a letter to Mr Whiteley in April 1920:

'Mr Bede, in a letter to me spoke about the Uncle Pearson suggesting the names for my pets. You know that couldn't have been for you know Henry cared nothing for learning — and the names he suggested for my pets were Mike and Tom and Jerry instead of the funny ones I gave them. He always said the names I gave to my pets were queer ones that didn't have any sense in them. Of course he said it in a kindly way. And also Mr Bede spoke of Henry Pearson's interesting me in the natural science studies.

But, Papa, he never told me the name of a flower, nor a bird, nor a tree. He liked the out-of-doors but it didn't make a difference to him whether a bird was a sparrow or a wren. He just liked the out-of-doors. I early learned I could not learn from him the things I wanted to find out about natural science.'

Her diary leaves no doubt that she believed that the source

of her knowledge and love of nature was her Angel Father:

'When I was coming back from the house of Elsie I did look looks about as I did go along. I saw a piece of bark. I did turn it over with care. There were ants. I made a set-down to watch them. Some ants carry bundles with queer looks. Big Jud at school says they are ant eggs.

I have not think so. They be too big for ant eggs — and I have remembers that Angel Father did call them nymphs de fourmis.'

She saw with the eye and mind of a scientist and the heart of a poet; strange qualities for the child of a lumberman.

'This woods is grey in winter when come cold days. And grey shadows walk among the trees. They touch one's face with velvet fingers when one goes walking in the woods.

In winter old grey leaves grow to look like lace. They are very beautiful. As I did go along, I saw many grey rocks. Some grey rocks had grey and green patches on them. Some of these patches had ruffles all round their edges. The grey patches on grey rocks are lichens. My Angel Father said so. Lichen folk talk in grey tones. And the things they say are their thoughts about the gladness of a winter day. I put my ear close to the rocks and I listen. This is how I do hear what they are saying. Then I do take a reed for a flute. I climb on a stump — on the most high stump that is near. I pipe on the flute to the wind what the lichens are saying. I am piper for the lichens that dwell on the grey rocks, and the lichens that cling to the trees grown old.'

10.

If the *Diary* was not written, as Opal claims, when she was a young child, it must have been composed before she was twenty two, her age at the time of publication. The suggestion that she made alterations and additions while she was piecing it together is ruled out by Ellery Sedgwick's assertion that this was impossible since he and his family were constantly with her while she was sorting and preparing the manuscript.

He wrote, in a letter to Constant Huntington in November 1920:

'At the time of her first visit, Opal Whiteley was living with two maiden ladies in Cambridge, Massachusetts. She was suffering from a lame back, which she subsequently ascribed to an attempted assault on her while living in Los Angeles, where she had undoubtedly endured with courage and extraordinary determination many privations and adventures. Her cash resources were something over twenty dollars. I gave her a little money to buy better food, and soon after her manuscript arrived from Los Angeles, made arrangements that she should live at the house of my mother-in-law, Mrs Walter C Cabot, of Brookline, who for many years has been obliged to keep to her bed. The household consisted of three trained nurses and three family servants, besides the men on the place. In Brookline Opal lived in comfort a hard-working and retired life. I saw her very frequently. My brother and sister-in-law, Mr and Mrs H B Cabot, saw her constantly. We were all intensely interested, and although I was not present when the boxes which held the precious manuscript were opened, as I was when the second consignment arrived, I did see and study the fragments, and throughout the whole winter made it a practice to pay visits to her while she was at work.

The method of work was this: as soon as Opal pieced a sheet completely she placed the fragments composing it into an envelope, and on the outside of this envelope wrote in long hand the passage it contained. This passage Opal would subsequently copy on a sheet. When she brought or sent to the office a number of these separate passages, one of my personal secretaries, Miss Gertrude E Tompson, in whom I have entire reliance, would copy them upon separate library cards.

Subsequently these cards would be sorted by Opal into a continuous narrative, and then recopied by Miss Tompson and submitted to Opal for final correction. During this process Miss Tompson spent a great deal of time working with Opal over the manuscript. She, as well as I and many other friends and witnesses, followed the whole performance carefully.

The work went very smoothly until February, when before the publication of the first chapters of the diary in the March *Atlantic* Opal received a letter from Mr Whiteley, saying in substance that the story reaching him from Boston that she was describing herself as the daughter of another was 'stuff.' The letter showed illiteracy, and was so curiously worded as rather to confirm than impair my confidence in Opal.'

There are only two other possible explanations. Either she was not the child of Mr and Mrs Whiteley and had, in fact, a background and upbringing far removed from that in which she spent the latter part of her childhood, for, if the *Diary* is genuinely the work of a child, it is difficult indeed to believe that she was their daughter; or else, the alternative, the fact that she was a most unusually sensitive and highly imaginative child made it possible for her to build out of the unlikely circumstances of her childhood in the forest a world of remarkable fantasy, and to make herself believe it to such an extent that she could convey this conviction to the readers of her diary.

Elbert Bede believed that the diary was written, or rewritten, during the time that she was in California, when she would have been about twenty years old, and that there she studied French and gathered together the knowledge of the historical and literary figures whose names she gave to her pets in the diary; but if one is going to believe that Opal wrote the diary at this age one has first of all to accept that she conceived the strange idea of producing a hoax, which she intended to pass off as the work of a child. Then she must have gone to the immense labour of printing thousands of words in childish capitals, taking care to spell most of them incorrectly, and to alter the character of her writing as she went along, for it will be remembered that Sedgwick described the change in handwriting in the diary from the childish capitals of the beginning to the gradually forming adult hand — and indeed, this is evident in the scraps of the diary that are in the present writer's possession. Having done this, she must have torn up each page, and finally pieced it all together again. This seems more difficult to believe than the simple story.

Inez Fortt, librarian to the University in Eugene, wrote:

'Whether she really wrote the diary as a small child, whether she really is the exiled daughter of French royalty, may not be known for sure. It is easy to dismiss her claims as ludicrous, but those who had investigated her life story most thoroughly are the least sure. What she claims is conceivable, even if dubious. Opal herself is the only one who speaks with absolute certainty.

"The diary is just as I printed it as a child seven and eight years old. There were no additions."'

Many people who knew her testified to her honesty. A superintendent of schools in Cottage Grove, James E Dunton, from 1912 to 1916, when Opal was a pupil in high school there, wrote:

'There is not a doubt in my mind but that Opal was telling the truth.' He went on: 'She seemed to be forever absorbed in her studies. She was an imaginative child, but perfectly truthful.'

Certain critics have made out that by elaborate scheming, and driven by ambition, Opal deliberately deceived *The Atlantic* into accepting a hoax. Those who knew her well acquit her of any such motives. Some even account for her strange behaviour by describing her as a psychic phenomenon. The Reverend W A Elkins, Minister of the Monmouth Christian church, who baptized Opal and in whose Sunday School she taught, wrote:

'Her strange adventure of life is the product of her own imagination. She is obsessed by an idea, and that idea is the outgrowth of her extremely active imagination. My personal observation of Opal prompts me to believe in her as a sincere, intense and highly gifted young woman. The inference has been left by some that she has made use of clever intrigue, but it is scarcely reasonable to believe that mere cleverness could take her so completely out of a more or less commonplace environment into the far distant environment of her particular fancy. Opal's dream has materialised. It may be true that her amazing career has been a demonstration of the fact that imagination sets into action physic *(sic.* psychic?) forces the extent and importance of which we can but vaguely guess.'

There were some who even saw in Opal's story a battle waged between the Catholic Church and the Devil himself. An article in the *Catholic Women's Review* for March 19th 1935, read:

'In Opal Whiteley we have a glimpse of the perfection of which nature in an ideal child may be capable. May we not feel that the appearance of so much beauty and grace aroused the ire of "the wicked spirits who wander about the earth for the ruin of souls" and that, with all the limited might that evil may possess, they plotted for its confusion?'

Much can be found in the diary itself to support the belief that it was written in childhood.

A leading american lawyer stated that, in her opinion, there is much internal evidence within the diary itself (its length and consistency, for example) to prove its authenticity. She said that murder convictions are often made on less evidence than surrounds the diary.

There is the quality of immediacy in the writing, which is characteristic of young children. It is in the nature of a running commentary. One feels that Opal came in from the woods and wrote down at once all she had seen and experienced while it was still fresh in her mind:

'The wind was calling. His calling was to little wood-folk and me. He did call more again: "Come petite Françoise, go explores." He was in a rush. I raced. Brave Horatius ran. We played tag with the wind.

By and by we came to a log. It was a nice little log. It was as long as three pigs as long as Peter Paul Rubens (her pet pig). I climbed upon it. I so did to look more looks about. The wind did blow in a real quick way. He made music all around. I danced on the log. When we were come to the house of Dear Love, they were standing by the steps. The husband of Dear Love did bring home to her a little nest that was in a tree that they did fall in the far woods today. The husband of Dear Love did think these little birds were most ready to fly from the nest when the tree did fall today. All the six little birds but one did get death as the tree did fall. They were such little things when we did take them out. The one live one was hungry. And we did feed him. We did feed him little bits at a time — a little bit of egg that was left in the dinner pail of the husband of Dear Love, did give to this little bird some satisfaction feels. Dear Love did cuddle it warm in her hands, and her husband did make the piece of egg into little divides for me to give to it. It did open its mouth most wide. And every time I did drop a piece of egg in the mouth of the little bird, I did open my mouth wide, too, from seeing the bird do it.'

This surely was not recollected in tranquillity. It had not passed through the screen of time and maturity but resembles the running commentary which is frequently the accompaniment to children's activities. Opal comments on what impresses her at the time, and from the point of view of a child, remembering vividly the small details which would be real to her at the time they happened, but would fade with the years. If the *Diary* were written in adolescence these would not have been the impressions remembered and recorded.

What a living picture she gives, in the clearly remembered details and in so few words:

'When we were come to the end of the lane there was the gate. It did take some long time to get it open. The plug did stick so tight and more yet. I did pull and I made more pulls. It came out. It did come out in a quick way. I got up in a slow way.'

Here again are the details that would be vivid at the time:

'After I did put the four new portraits in the old log I did follow a path that leads to a path that goes to the house of Elsie. Elsie was making for her young husband a whipped-cream cake. She was stirring things together in the most big yellow bowl. She did stir them in a quick way.'

And again, here is Opal recording exactly what she did to her sunbonnet in the way a child remembers and reproduces the simple details of an action just performed:

'I didn't put my sunbonnet back on my head again, but I did give the strings a little tie in front so it wouldn't come off again,' and here are the details of lacing up one's shoes:

'I drew my toes away from the water and let the sun dry my feet so I could put my stockings on. When I did have my shoes most laced up to the top, I gave the strings a tuck in and started on.'

Here she is describing the feeling of soft mud between the toes, an experience of delight essentially childlike, but one which fades with the years:

'Today is more rain come again. I like rain. I like the music patters it does make. I like to have feels of it on my head. When it rains I like to go barefooted. I like to feel the clean mud by the lane ooze up between my toes.'

Here is the young child's hazy idea of the passing of time, when an hour can seem endless:

'The mamma is hours and hours gone now.'

Opal's account of her loose tooth takes one back immediately to seven-year-old days, to the forgotten feeling when one's tongue would not leave the waggling tooth alone:

'One of my tooths is loose and a queer feel. It was funny feels — its being loose.'

Surely it is a child who is describing the ritual of pulling it out. Even the colour of the string to be used is important:

'After I did eat some of my mush, I did go to the stringbox and I pulled out a string. It was a white one. There was lots of white string in that box, and a pink one and a green one. I put the white string back and I pulled out the green one. I did tie the one part of it around my tooth with carefuls. Then I did come a walk over to where the broom stands behind the back door. I did tie the other end of the long green string to the broom-handle. And I kept hold of the middle of the string in my hand so when the broom had falls it wouldn't give a bump to my tooth when it did pull it out. I went a walk off. The tooth didn't come out. The green string did just have a slip off the broom-handle.'

After a further unsuccessful attempt, she says:

'Then I thought I'd wait until after dinner. I took the string off my tooth, but I left it on the door knob to remind me to do it after dinner.'

Then comes a description of a visit to the woods, during which she refers once or twice to the tooth, and at length she goes home to the green string and successfully pulls out the tooth. It is her last remark that seems to put the very stamp of childhood on to the account. When the tooth is finally out she says, 'Then I did do the green string up in a roll. I am going to keep it.' It is a most unusual grown-up, or adolescent, looking back to such an incident over the years, who would say, of the string that had performed this important task, 'I am going to keep it,' but how exactly right it is for a child.

There are many indications in the *Diary* of the size of the writer. She tries to manage a full size broom and finds that it does not behave for her as it does for the mamma:

'First I swept the floors in a careful way. The broom made bobby moves. That broom in my hands makes not moves like the moves it does make in the hands of the mamma. It has so much of tallness. I look up its handle.'

She was small enough to be taken on someone's knee when she was in need of comforting:

'When sleeps was come upon the mamma's baby, — (why not 'my baby sister'?) — I straightaway did go in a hurry to the house of Dear Love by the mill by the far woods. Dear Love, she did lead me back into her house and did have me to sit on a chair. I sat on its corner. And I felt lumps come up in my throat. She did take off my fascinator, and she did take off my shoes so my feet would get dry. Then she did take me on her lap and did ask me what was the matter.'

The baby was heavy for her to carry about:

'This baby has likes for many things. It does have such likes to be rocked. The mamma does have me to rock it and teter it on the bed and walk the floor with it. Sometimes it does get most heavy. Then I do let my knees bend under and I do sit on the floor and rock it back and forth.'

It is surely a cynic who can say that this simple clear word picture is the writing of an adult.

The papa's coat swept the floor behind her when she put it on:

'Today in the morning, when the mamma was in the other room, I did take down from its hook the papa's big coat. I did put it on to me and it did trail away out behind.'

She climbed up, as small children do, to find out what she wanted to know:

'Today was dyeing day. In the boiler was beautiful blue water. I know because I climbed on the stove-hearth and peeked in.'

When she could not get the animals out of their pens to 'go explores' because the chore boy had repaired the fences, she took 'Cathedral Service' outside, but she was not tall enough to see over the top of the fences:

'After some long time, when we did all get settled down to quietness I did start service. After the third hymn I did preach the morning sermon. I did choose for my text, "I will lift up mine eyes to the hills," I had to peek through the pig-pen to do it, for it did have more tallness than I did have.'

She was small enough to hide her head in a grown-up's apron, when she felt in need of consolation and to remember the soapy smell it had on washing days:

'When I was come to the house of Sadie McKibben, she was washing clothes. On wash-days along in the afternoon her hair does hang in strings about her face. And her nice blue gingham apron with the cross-stitches on it does have rumples and soapy smells. I do know so for I do smell those soapy smells when I cuddle close to her apron on wash-days.'

Making butter and lifting the field gate were heavy tasks for her:

'Some days there is cream to be shaked into butter. When there is only a little cream to be shaked into butter, then the mamma has me to shake it to and fro in a glass jar. Sometimes it gets awfully heavy and my arms do get ache feels up and down.

We went our way to the pasture-bars. I did give to one a push, and it made a drop down. Then I give two more pushes, and they went drop downs. We went on through in between.

It took a more long time to fix up the pasture-bars. They have so heavy feels when I go to put them back again.'

It is a remarkable adolescent or adult who can remember how heavy the bars of a field gate feel, vividly enough to record it like this many years later.

From time to time the Whiteley family moved from one lumber camp to another. Before one of these moves Opal tells how she collected together and made a list of her 'necessary things.'

'Moving is a bit amount of problem. But mostly now I do have my prepares done. I am going to take with me when we goes to the mill just my necessary things — the mamma says none but my necessary things can go. She said that was my blue calico apron and my grey calico apron and the clothes that go under them and my two pairs of stockings and the shoes I have on and my sunbonnet and my slate and Cyr's Reader.'

But Opal had other possessions, of great importance to her: 'I have some more necessary things that the mamma has not knows of. There is my two books that Angel Mother and Angel Father did write in and I do study in every day, and the pictures of grandmère and grandpère and tante and tante and oncle and all the others that I do love much every day.'

This is characteristic of a child's way of making a list. One sees her mentally ticking off each of the pictures of 'tante and tante and oncle.' There is no need to name them as an older, more self-conscious writer would have done. Opal knows quite well which is which, and that is sufficient.

This is followed by another essentially childlike list of things she has collected, all significant to her, but to a grown up, so much rubbish:

'And there is seven of the tail feathers of Lars Porsena (the pet crow) — that he did lose when he did lose his tail. And there is four old horse-shoes of William Shakespeare that the blacksmith did have allows for me to have when he was putting new shoes on to William Shakespeare. And there is the thimble of Dear Love that she has given me to carry drinks to the folks in the hospital. And there is Elsie's baby's little old shoe that got worn out and she gave it to me for Nanerl Mozart to sleep in.'

Had Opal written this when she was older, looking back, would she not have written 'the thimble of Dear Love that she gave me' not, 'has given.' 'Has given' surely means it has just happened. The list goes on:

'And there is the egg-shells Ben Jonson and Sir Francis Bacon and Pius VII and Nicholas Boileau and Edmund Spenser and Oliver Goldsmith and John Fletcher and Francis Beaumont and Cardinal Richelieu and Sir Walter Raleigh and the rest of Minerva's chickens hatched out of. And there is the skins of the caterpillars they did grow too big for when they were growing into papillons and phalenes.'

11.

Opal tells of the death of one of her school friends, Lola. She gives a simple and poignant account of how the child lay still in a white dress, while the children gathered round and sang. It is clear that she does not fully understand what has happened, but in the characteristic way of young children her attention is quickly distracted from what she does not understand. She sees a butterfly and then a wasp fetching mud for its nest. These are real for her and have more meaning than the appearance of death.

'And there was Brave Horatius by the steps, and I saw a yellow butterfly and a little way away there was a mud puddle. By the mud puddle was a guêpe. She came. She went. Every time she did come she did take a bit of mud. I did watch. And I had seeing she was making a cradle of mud for a baby guêpe to be.

Then I went a little way back. I saw a white butterfly. I have wonders if Lola will wear her white silk dress to school when fall-time is come. I looked more looks about. Among the grasses on a little bush there was a katydid. Its wings, they were folded close. And it was washing its front feet.'

Another passage illustrates this same childlike quality, the ability to be quickly distracted from what one does not fully understand:

'And while I did have watches of the plant-folks that dwell about the moss-box, and while I did have listens of the songs in the tree-tops, then it was the pensée girl with the far away look in her eyes and the man of the long step that whistles most all of the time did come walking through the woods. I had sees there was joy-lights in her eyes, and the looks he looked at her was like the looks the young husband of Dear Love does look at her when he is come home from work at eventime. And I did reach out my arms above them for blessings to come.

They had not knows of my reaching out my arms above them. They did just have sees for one another. I have sure feels they didn't see that green caterpillar having sleeps under the green hazel leaf. He did take out a ring of gold, and he did tell her what was his mother's wedding ring; and the caterpillar that was asleep did have wake-ups, and he crawled a little more under the hazel leaf.

He did kiss her again. Last year I had more green caterpillars like unto this one. And they did grow and change and they was very big brown moths with velvet wings and velvet feet. And he did say, "I want to help you to have all the love joy in the world." And the fat green caterpillar fell off the leaf away down on the ground.'

To Opal the caterpillar was as important, and worthy of her close observation, as the young couple and the account, in its naiveté and total freedom from sentimentality is essentially childlike.

She was fully aware of the meaning of death when it took away her pets and she felt in her own body the fall of a loved fir tree. Her descriptions of these are deeply moving and there is a poignancy in her writing of the death of her friend, 'the girl who has no seeing' which carries great conviction. She gains her effect with sheer simplicity and with the directness of a child. There is no sophisticated use of language, no extravagance, no straining to impress. S L Bensusan wrote of these accounts:

'If the experiences had not reached the heart of the child they could never have been set out as they are here.'

Of her description of the death of William Shakespeare, the old horse, she wrote: 'No trained writer, however gifted, could originate a passage like that. If we examine the most touching passages we shall find that they are reached with the most rigid economy of means, the utmost simplicity of expression.'

Of the death of her special pet pig, Peter Paul Rubens, Opal wrote: 'I am feeling all queer inside. Yesterday was butchering day. Among the hogs they butchered was Peter Paul Rubens. The mamma let me go off to the woods all day, after my morning's work was done. Brave Horatius and Lars Porsena of Clusium went with me — a part of the time he perched on my shoulder, and then he would ride on the back of Brave Horatius. Felix Mendelssohn rode in my apron pocket and Elizabeth Barret Browning followed after.

We had not gone far when we heard an awful squeal — so different from the way pigs squeal when they want their supper. I felt cold all over. Then I did have knowings why the mamma had let me start away to the woods without scolding. And I ran a quick run to save my dear Peter Paul Rubens; but already he was dying — and he died with his head in my lap. I sat there feeling dead, too, until my knees were all wet with blood from the throat of my dear Peter Paul Rubens. After I changed my clothes and put the bloody ones in the rain barrel, I did go to the woods to look for the soul of Peter Paul Rubens. I didn't find it, but I think when comes the spring I will find it among the flowers — probably in the blossom of a faon lily or in the top of a fir tree. To-day when Brave Horatius and I went through the woods we did feel its presence near. When I was come back from the woods they made me grind sausage, and every time I did turn the handle I could hear that little pain squeal Peter Paul Rubens always gave when he did want me to come where he was at once.'

The references to her early life with her Angel Father and Mother are scattered through the diary, and all slight, but when one begins to put them together they fall into a pattern which is consistent, and convinces by its very lightness of touch. Opal has no need to enlarge on what she knew so well; she was not writing for an audience for whom such references might need explanation. She writes of her memories as they return to her in her loneliness, and for herself:

'There are no rows and rows of books in this house, like Angel Mother and Angel Father had. There is only three books here. One is a cook-book and one is a doctor-book and one is an almanac. They are all on the top of the cupboard most against the top of the house. They have not interest names on their backs.

No one hereabouts does call things by the names Angel Father did. Sometimes I do have thinks this world is a different world to live in. I do have lonesome feels.

This day — it was a lonely day. I did have longings all its hours for Angel Mother and Angel Father. In between times all day at school I did print messages for them on grey leaves I did gather on the way to school. I did tell on the leaves the longings I was having. And I did print on more leaves how I do read out of the books they did make — how I do sit in the manger and read what is in them.'

Surely this can find an echo in the mind of anyone who even faintly remember his or her own childhood and the intenseness with which one felt. She goes on:

'The glad song in my heart sings not bright today. It is lonesome feels I have. But I do try to have thinks as how I can bring happiness to folks about. That is such a help when lonesome feels do come. Angel Mother did say, "Make earth glad, little one, that is the way to keep the fire-tongue of the glad song ever in your heart. It must not go out." I so do try to keep it there. I so do try, for it is helps on cold days and old days. And I did have remembers as how it was Angel Mother did say, "When one keeps the glad song singing in one's heart then do the hearts of others sing."'

To believe that a memory like this is the product of a child's imagination is to assume a most remarkable child but, whatever the truth may be, here is a child's reaction to loneliness and lack of sympathy, whether real or imagined, most poignant in its sincerity and simplicity.

Whatever the original cause which made Opal believe in her Angel Parents, it is undisputed that, as the years passed, the idea became more and more a part of her. Many years after she had left her home in Oregon and was living in England, she wrote to Lady Grey:

'My Angel Mother held the thought that those who came for a time to be with one — even only for a few hours or days were great souls whose destiny was linked with one's own and who watched over one — for she often felt that death was but a gate — and that we were greater in death than in life — that one is released from the earth-bound body and the soul is more free to guard with its love those whom it loves — that is, that the guarding power of those who have loved us and who have gone away is very strong about us.'

In letters to Constant Huntington she speaks of the pet name which her mother had for her. The English edition of her *Diary* had a fleur-de-lys on the cover of her book. She wrote:

'I am so pleased with the tiny fleur-de-lys. It is like a signature too. It happens to be one of my mother's pet names for me.'

She wrote to Huntington about her visit to Vienna and their old home:

'The dear sweet things about Vienna was that I met there again some of the kind people I had known as a child. Grandma said I found so much in Vienna because I brought it back in my heart. (Which Grandma told her this? Was it the Duchess of Chartres? If so did it indicate her acceptance of Françoise?) It was such a dear historic house we lived in, it was filled with the shadows of the past, memories of the whole Empire.'

12.

It has been suggested that Opal, being so firmly convinced of the truth about her parentage, may have revised her original diary, interpolating references to her Angel Father and Mother which, when discovered, would substantiate her claims. Elbert Bede believed that such revision was carried out during the time that she was in Los Angeles, but, like all the rest of the strange and bewildering story, there is no proof that this was done, and it is probable that the question will forever remain unanswered. The references to her Angel parents are woven into the diary and lightly and almost casually mentioned. Surely, if this had been a conscious intention, she would have made her points more strongly and left no doubt of the evidence which could prove her story.

Whether the Whiteley family was her real one or not there is no doubt that Opal was vividly out of tune with her home. It is significant that she never speaks of the Whiteley household as 'home,' it is always 'the house we live in;' Mrs Whiteley is called 'the mamma;' even the baby is referred to as 'the mamma's baby.' Certainly she had little in common with the Whiteleys. For consolation she turned to the animals of the farm and the creatures of the woods, whom she watched with close and loving attention, living an intense life of her own in their company, finding an outlet for her feelings in her secret diary:

'I made little vases out of clay. I put them in the oven to

bake. The mamma found my vases of clay. She threw them out the window. When I went to pick them up, they were broken. I felt sad inside. I went to talk things over with my chum, Michael Angelo Sanzio Raphael.

He is that most tall fir tree that grows just back of the barn. It is such a comfort to nestle up to Michael Angelo Sanzio Raphael when one is in trouble. He is such a grand tree. He has an understanding soul.'

The mamma must have found her strange child quite beyond her understanding. Her reaction to her incomprehensible behaviour was generally a spanking. After one of these Opal wrote,

'I don't think I'll print more tonight. I printed this sitting on the wood-box where the mamma put me after she spanked me after I got home with the milk. The back part of me feels a little bit sore, but I am happy listening to the twilight music of God's good world. I'm real glad I'm alive.' She goes on, 'Now I think I shall go out the bedroom window and talk to the stars. They always smile so friendly.' In spite of all, she is able to say,

'This is a very wonderful world to live in.'

'Morning is glad on the hills,' she wrote. 'The sky sings in blue tones. The earth sings in green. I am so happy. The mamma has gone for a visit away. Before her going she did set me to remind the baby. I do so. In-between times I print, and I do spell over and over the words in my two books Angel Father and Angel Mother did make. I sing-song the letters of the words when I go adown the road. So I do when I am in the house when the mamma isn't at home. I do not so when she is at home because she won't let me.'

The world of adults was beyond Opal's comprehension. Jenny Strong came to visit and Opal told her that the ruffles round her neck were like the ruffles round the neck of the man with the glove, when Titian made his picture. Jenny Strong did not take this in the spirit that Opal had intended.

'She looked a queer look and she said to the mamma, "What a naughty child!"' Opal was sent to crawl under the bed and to stay there. She had her own way of dealing with the incomprehensible treatment; she confided to her diary:

'I have wonders about folks. They are hard to understand. I have thinks I will just say a little prayer. My. I do have such hungry feels now. They at the table are not through yet. I make swallows down my throat. It is most hard not to eat what I have saved for my animal friends. But they will like it — so I can wait waits until breakfast time. I can. In between times I will have thinks and prayers.'

Out of tune with the Whiteley home, Opal responded with all the warmth of her nature to the few in her circle who showed her understanding and kindness: Sadie McKibben, who may have been the wife of the mill owner, Dear Love and her young husband and the man who wears grey neckties and is kind to mice. Her portraits of these give a picture of a remarkable community, bound together by the hardness of their life and yet retaining a sensitivity to the life of the forest and to a child. Opal's response to them and her quiet acceptance of the harsh treatment from Mrs Whiteley as inevitable, but beyond her understanding, ring true of the reactions of a child to the incomprehensible world of grown-ups:

'When I got to the end she did spank me again. She said that was to be good on. Now I do think it was real kind of her to tell me what the last spanking was for.

Most times I don't know what I get spanked for. And I do like to know because if I did have knows what I was spanked for, I'd be real careful about doing what it was again, if it was not helping folks of the fields and woods. I have to do that no matter how many spanks I do get for it.'

In *The Fairyland Around Us* Opal gives a different picture of the Whiteley home. She is still spanked, but there is no mention of Angel parents. She writes of an Uncle who tells her stories of his childhood experiences with animals and of 'my dear little Great-Grandmother who is my own dear Mamma's father's mother.'

It is difficult to reconcile the two accounts unless she felt that the book she was writing for children, with the intention of publication, could not reveal her true feelings about the Whiteleys, where her private diary, which she had no intention of publishing, could safely contain her secret thoughts.

Perhaps as telling as anything else when one is considering the age of the author is the hazy line that is drawn in the diary between fact and fantasy. In the way of a child groping its slow way from the world of fantasy to the world of reality, she writes, almost in the same sentence, of her careful, accurate observations of nature, and of fairies. It is possible also that, unaware even herself of what she is doing, she mixes inextricably her records of actual happenings with the strange weavings of her own extraordinarily active and fertile imagination.

There are two further pieces of evidence for the authenticity of the diary. One is provided by the materials of the diary themselves, the fragments of paper on which it was written and the crayons Opal used. Some of these scraps, with their letters in coloured pencil, were examined microscopically by a graphologist and the verdict given is of great interest. Some at least of the paper itself appeared to be of a particular kind which was manufactured only before the first World War. The graphologist stated:

'When examined by transmitted light all the specimens and scraps of paper submitted for examination have a more irregular pattern of thickness of texture, when compared with samples of modern wrapping paper. The crayons,' he said, 'were of unusually good quality, such as would only be available in a period of prosperity, as that before 1914.' It would have been impossible, therefore, for Opal to fabricate even parts of the diary as a young adult, unless she had kept some of the original wrapping paper and crayons, carrying them about with her on her travels from place to place, which seems exceedingly unlikely. Not only this, but examination of the fragments under the microscope revealed that they had been exposed, at some time, to the effect of damp and weather — evidence which corroborates Opal's statement that the pages of the diary were hidden in the woods. The paper, in most cases, had been folded before being written on, and where it had been cut there was evidence that small scissors had been used and the scissor movement frequently repeated. 'This,' the graphologist said, 'would imply the clumsiness of the child using scissors at an early age.' No evidence here of 'large sheets of white typing paper' such as Elbert Bede accused her of using in Los Angeles.

Round some of the pages Opal has drawn a heavy line, as a kind of frame, within which she has written. When she reached the edge of this frame, even if in the middle of a word, she broke off and continued again from the left hand edge. The result of this is that much of the diary was difficult to decipher. This framing, or enclosing of writing or drawing, is frequently a feature of the work of children who feel themselves to be insecure; they make for themselves a framework or fence to surround and protect them from the world. The fact that Opal did this not only seems to confirm that the pages are the work of a child, but to suggest a childhood of insecurity and unhappiness, in keeping with her own accounts of her early years.

It will be remembered that Opal published *The Fairyland Around Us* a short time before the *Diary* appeared. This she is known to have written some time between the ages of twelve and twenty-two. It is in part in the form of a diary and it is clear from the similarity of style and outlook that it came from the same author as the childhood *Journal*. There is, however, a marked distinction between the two books. *The Fairyland Around Us* has not the life and sparkle of the earlier *Diary*, the spontaneity and vividness, the truly child-like quality of which makes it unique.

This loss of freshness which characterizes the book which

Opal is known to have written as an adolescent between twelve and twenty-two, seems to give the final proof that the first diary was composed when she was much younger. The creative work of young children, in painting and in writing almost invariably passes through such a stage. Their first expressions are often fresh as morning, then the dew dries off the grass, clouds cover the sun and the first sparkle is gone.

The Foreword to *The Fairyland Around Us* calls it 'a notable achievement for a girl of twenty.' Among the quotations at the beginning of the book Opal has included one which, seen in the perspective of her own life, seems particularly apposite. It is from Mencius:

'The great man is he who does not lose his child's heart.'

13.

One cannot, however, entirely rule out the possibility that the *Diary* is a fraud. It was put together some time before 1919, when Opal was about twenty. Given someone of her nature and character, to fabricate a story of this kind could be a way of achieving what she so desired and needed — recognition. But the more one reads the *Diary* the less inclined one becomes to believe that this is the truth. Elbert Bede puts forward a strong case against her, but all her story, particularly her later life, was not known to him. It seems that in the early days he was her friend and support and once wrote,

'Opal is utterly without guile and anyone who really knows her must agree that if she says she wrote the diary at a certain age it is the truth.' It is interesting to speculate on the reasons for his change of attitude.

Bede gives the impression that Opal only made use of her friends, chiefly to provide her with money, but many people testified to their feelings of kindliness and affection towards her. Mrs Creighton, writing in November 1929, said:

'One thing in her favour is that though I have had her staying with me, she has never asked me for a penny tho' I know she is desperately hard up. Her one desire is to earn her living by writing.'

There is no doubt that she endeared herself to many people, but the kindest amongst them found her far from easy. Constant Huntington wrote to her in January 1933:

'I wish you could cease to be a mystery woman and become just an ordinary princess.'

A letter I received from an American who knew Opal when he was seven, shows clearly the affection which she inspired, an affection which, in his case at least, lasted half a century. It also throws interesting light on the controversial question of Opal's relationship with Mr and Mrs Whiteley:

'I remember Opal from when I was seven and we lived in Cottage Grove, Oregon. Her parents were mean to her, which is the reason my mother took an interest in her and tried to help her. Our whole family had complete confidence in her as she was never known to lie in the least, and as my mother always said, was the most guileless person she ever knew.

Opal wrote to my mother quite frequently. My mother told me many things she wrote, among which was that she had been accepted by the Archduchess Maria Dorothea.

I have many fond recollections of Opal and I am most sorry that she has had so much trouble. She is truly the only one, no other could be like her.'

Professor Lee Thorndyke of Columbia University, described as one of the greatest living psychologists, stated that no evidence or argument could shake his conviction that the diary was written in childhood, because it would be impossible for a grown-up person to have composed it, and certainly one feels, as one reads it, that — like the Gospels — if one had intended to make the whole thing up, one would not have gone about it in that way.

There is the testimony of many people who believed sincerely in the truth of the diary. Viscount Grey maintained his belief in the book even after doubts had been cast on its authenticity, and wrote to Huntington in December 1929:

'I see no reason whatever to doubt her *bona fides.* My wife and my youngest stepson, when they were in America, saw the actual pieces of the diary.' (This was Stephen Tennant. He wrote to me, 'I remember so well my stepfather's delight in the Opal Whiteley Diaries — he *adored* them.') As to her connection with the Orleans family she is, I am sure, convinced of this herself, but I have no means of knowing the evidence of it. The connection was apparently acknowledged by, at any rate, one member of the family, but is repudiated by others.'

From early days she impressed people with her sincerity. The Cottage Grove *Sentinel*, writing of her in May 1915, said:

'She has a most remarkable face, not only for its unusual beauty, but for its innocence, its intelligence and its eagerness. Miss Whiteley's life should prove an inspiration to the growing generation,' and Bede, writing of her in 1933, said:

'First impressions of Opal always were that she was exotic, sincere, intensely religious, unusually considerate of others, anxious to do things to bring joy to others, affectionate but fluttery. Often Opal seemed a thing from the world apart — and she herself seemed to forget her presence here. That she often, in her childhood days, climbed into trees and fell to the ground while dreaming or in a trance, is well authenticated.'

Her professor at the University, Dr W D Smith, believed her to be sincere and James Hargrove, a close friend at the time when the *Diary* first appeared, wrote to her:

'The fact is that if you were to swear tomorrow that you had composed the diary three or four years ago it would not in the least change my conviction that you wrote it when you were a small child, at the time of the events described in it.'

A letter from James Townsend, written from Los Angeles in May 1923, says:

'I have stored for Miss Whiteley quite a number of her beautiful book, *The Fairyland Around Us*. She was a remarkable girl and I regretted very much to see the suspicion thrown upon her work. The genuineness of her diary as a child production is convincing to us who knew her while she was in Los Angeles. The diary was in fragments and was shipped to her from Hollywood by the daughter of Mr William M Gentle, who is in my office.'

S L Bensusan gave his opinion:

'It may be that since the diary was put together for publication there have been slight emendations, trifling concessions to popularity, but that the book is in the main quite genuine I incline strongly to believe.'

Sedgwick himself said, in a letter to the *Portland Oregonian:*

'It is too much to hope, of course, that all people will believe in the authenticity of the diary, but I have come to believe in the authenticity of the manuscript because of the overwhelming testimony which confronts all of us who have worked with it.'

And he wrote to Barbara Ward, Editor of *The Economist:*

'On the genuineness of the story printed in the *Atlantic* I will stake my absolute conviction. An almost incredible amount of evidence is fresh in my memory. The scene, when I first introduced the passionate little lover of birds and beasts to Sir Edward Grey, was one of the most interesting I ever witnessed and my whole intimate association with the child from Fairyland was a revelation of what a child's mind can be.'

He puts his finger here on what is of primary importance in any assessment of the diary and for which alone, a book such as the present one can be justified, not whether it was written in early childhood or at some later age, but its importance as a revelation of a child's mind.

A review in *The Observer* for September 1920 reads:

'The *Diary* of Opal Whiteley is a book full of beauty and equally full of meaning, whatever view may be taken of the precise history of its composition. It is a demonstration of Ruskin's doctrine that, so long as the imagination is right, nothing else matters.

It is a history blazoning forth much that ought to rivet the psychologist and the educator. That it is essentially the outcome of a real experience, one can cherish little doubt. At the same time its acceptance as an original record at the age described is attended with many difficulties.'

Inez Fortt has an interesting theory about the writing of the *Diary* which needs to be considered:

'The publication of *The Fairyland Around Us* had cost Opal all her savings and the point was reached when she ran out of money. The printer refused to continue and, to her dismay, destroyed all the plates. She collected the sheets that had been printed, and pasted in her own illustrations and captioned them in ink and had them bound, but the experience took its toll and she was ill. She seemed to have lost interest and energy, and for the first time she could no longer call upon her great will power to carry her through. It was at this time,' Inez Fortt wrote, 'that Opal "fell apart" — or rather she lived in two worlds, one as an adult, and the other as a child again in the woods with her little companions.' At this time Opal was a guest at the home of Mrs Maude Harwood Bales in Los Angeles. 'Opal spent her days and most of her evenings in her upstairs room where she closeted herself for long hours of writing,' Mrs Bales wrote later. One day Mrs Bales noticed that large sheets of paper were spread out on the bed with printed letters at least one inch high and with no spaces between the letters to form words. Could this have been the time Opal was writing her 'six-year-old' diary? I believe so. Confused and defeated, dependent on the generosity of friends and acquaintances, Opal probably withdrew from life about her. Only in her room was she able to 'lose' herself and forget the present. There she could relive a dream of the past, her childhood in the woods with the little animals who accompanied her on explorations, and where she had been a Princess in a Fairyland. And as she regressed in her mind to the past, she thought as a child and wrote as a child. She was no longer Opal Whiteley but a royal Princess. As she sat and printed, the dream and the reality fused together, and the child-princess and Opal became one.'

This is a theory to which the reader can give some credence, but there is no certainty that the sheets she was writing at that time were the diary. I have in my possession scraps of the original diary, written on pieces of wrapping paper and paper bags, as Ellery Sedgwick described them, and which show signs of having been exposed to weather, as she claims they were, when hidden in the woods. I believe there was an original diary, written in childhood, but perhaps less in quantity than the published *Journal*. It is possible that in putting it together in Boston she added, to this diary, material she had written later, perhaps in Los Angeles.

14.

Certainly it is known for a fact that she did keep a diary in childhood, that some of it at least was printed in capitals and written on scraps of paper, and that the paper was torn up and kept in a cardboard box. Elbert Bede wrote, in the *Sunday Oregonian* in November 1933, that he had confirmed these facts from someone who had seen the diary. Lord Grey and his wife and stepson had seen parts of the diary, similar to those I have myself. The question still remains, though, whether the *Journal* which eventually came to the *Atlantic* consisted wholly, or only in part, of the childhood diary. Bede was of the opinion that it was substantially rewritten in later years, but an adolescent is usually too close to childhood to be able to write in the style and thought of a child. An adult might perhaps be able to produce a style which is convincingly childlike, but anyone younger would find it very difficult.

Had the diary been the work of an adolescent, as Bede claims, it is reasonable to expect that it would show some awareness of and interest in sex, but in fact it is noticeably innocent in this respect, even in relation to the animals:

'The time is so long I have been praying prayers for Dear Love to have a baby soon. And now the angels have told her it's going to come in about five months. I have thinks that is quite a time long to wait waits.'

When she writes of the arrival of Elsie's baby it is hard to believe that such innocence was only assumed:

'Elsie has a brand-new baby and all the things that go with it. The baby — it is a beautiful baby — though it does have much redness of face from coming such a long way in the cold last night. Maybe it was the coldness of the night that did cause the angels to make the mistake. They stopped at the wrong house. I'm quite sure this is the very baby I have been praying for the angels to bring to the new young folks that do live by the mill by the far woods. Dear Love, her young husband does call her. And they are so happy. But they have been married seven whole months and haven't got a baby yet. And most all today I did feel I better tell Elsie as how this baby isn't her baby, before she does get too fond of it.'

At last Opal summons up enough courage to tell Elsie the bad news. The diary goes on:

'From the house of Elsie I did go to talk with Michael Angelo Sanzio Raphael. He does so understand. While I was telling him all about how the angels did make a mistake and did bring Dear Love's baby to the house of Elsie, I did hear a little voice. It was a baby voice. It did come from the barn. I went in to see. I slid down to the manger of the gentle Jersey cow. And with her was a dear new baby calf.

When I did ask the ranch folks when it was brought, they did say it was brought in the night last night. I have thinks the same angel that did bring the new baby to the house of Elsie did bring also in her other arm that baby calf to the gentle Jersey cow.'

The review in *The Observer* of September 1920 goes on,

'Whatever be the solution of these things, the main interest of the book in its vitality of imagination and its pregnancy of issues bearing upon child life remains unaffected. It will come as a windfall to all who believe that the neglect of the imagination and its potencies is the paramount error of educative systems.'

Those who have not forgotten their own childhood will probably agree that many children, perhaps most, are as sensitive as Opal. Some have as rich an imagination and a very few are able to put their thoughts and feelings into words. Opal had the gift of expression to a high degree which enabled her to reveal, through her diary, something of that inner world of childhood whose doors so rarely open to outsiders. Here is the heart of the whole matter, and in this lies the importance of the diary and its significance for all who have to do with children, the reminder which it gives of the simple but immensely important fact of the acute sensitivity of childhood and its revelation of the secret world in which so many children live.

If one is sceptical of the ability of a child to express herself as Opal does in the diary, it must be remembered that at the age of three she could already write — as other exceptional children have been known to do. It was reported that at six she talked like a grown-up and that she spent much time forming words and writing. Her Whiteley grandmother related that Opal had strange names for her pets and that she used to talk of the whisperings of her creatures, and of the wind and stars. Also, she was small for her age. In a photograph taken at school she appears to be very small. No one is certain of her date of birth. Could it be that she was actually a year or two older than everyone thought? If this is the case, and the diary was actually written when she was eight or nine, the doubt about her ability to write as she did is largely dispersed.

Even so, her writing may seem to be beyond the power of a young child, but, for comparison, here is some original writing by children of six and seven years. Punctuation and spelling, with certain characteristic exceptions, have been corrected:

'The sun smiles in dawn and in day and the squirrels, grey and red, dance under the sun's smile.'

'To the brain come forth the dream, with uncontrollable feats.'

'On Monday when I came home from school, I had deep thoughts about science. And how will man go to the moon? And how will man venture in unexplored seas? Then we had tea.'

'On Wednesday I thought about Nature, of how life started by the amoeba and of deep sea divers and bathyspheres and strange fishes like the coelocanth. You'll never catch the coelocanth and nature is very wonderful and amazing.'

'Yesterday I thought about the eclipse of the sun and science, mostly about rockets and space ships and space suits, and I am hoping to write a space magazine of future rockets and space ships. And I have heard that Russia is going to jet a rocket to Venus, and I have lots of future pictures in my mind, and I like the progress of space and I have read lots of books about it.'

'Our story begins in the time when there were no men and the world was overrun by evil. The devil had an emerald. This was no ordinary emerald. This was a magic emerald and it was very magical and the devil killed them and only evil men were left. So the evil men helped the devil and evil went on and on. But when Jesus Christ appeared the magic emerald was lost, but when Jesus died it was found again. But evil lives on in the house of the Prince of Death.'

'The trees are a tall, fat, twisted, cold spiky shape, with branches that stretch up to the sky.'

'Searing, black, shadowy trees.'

'Once God made a world. It is the same world that we live in today. First he made the dry land, and the sea, then the high mountains and the valleys, and the rivers, and the mosses by the water's edge, and the flowers and then the trees, and then fishes and animals, and then he made man and wife and children. Women were glad that God had given the world to them.'

This child, like Opal, heard trees and birds talking:

'The birds talked in the trees and the trees said to me, "The sun is in the sky."'

Here is the same respect as Opal's for the lives of all small creatures:

'It is just as important if an ant dies as if a person dies.'

And here is the same inconsequence of thought which characterizes Opal's writing. Notice also the use of 'did see' and 'did bring' instead of 'saw' and 'brought.'

I did see a blackbird on a post when I got up. It has a yellow bill — it looked nice to see him on the post and last night, as I pulled my tooth out, it did have a bit of blood inside it. I put it under my pillow but I did not see it when I looked. I think the fairies will come tonight. It is the first day of spring today and Glyn did bring a guinea pig to school. His name is Swip. It is a nice name for him.'

Here in this seven-year-old's treatment of a prosaic subject is the same freshness and touch of poetry which is found in Opal's diary:

'The body is something you really need to keep yourself alive. You know you can't live without your body, but I was just telling you. If you are deaf it is really such a pity, but you can read I know. If you have on some clothes, as I hope you have, you are all right, but if you have none on you feel cold. When you have your little teeth you have twenty-four, but when all your little teeth fall out and your big ones come you have thirty-two teeth. You breathe out of your nose. Now if you don't know that there are adnoses up your nose.

Your bones are very funny things. I don't know why but when you look at a scelington you see all the bones. Some go different ways and some don't.

When you fall over and cut yourself and it begins to bleed you lose some of your blood. That's why they have blood transfusions, so if you are kind enough to give a little of your blood it can save a lot of lives. In your fingers you have veins and if you cut your veins very badly you can die, if you lose enough blood. It is true you know.

When you eat your food it goes past your chest and some of it is stored in for a little while, and then when you go to the lavatree it comes out that had been stored. That is what comes out but what is still in there goes with the blood and makes more blood. That is how we live, through the years that have passed and the years that have got to pass.'

The following passage, written by a mentally handicapped boy of fifteen shows the same poetic quality and sensitivity that characterizes Opal's writing. It provokes the question: Would more children express their feelings and thoughts in poetic form if we only knew how to unlock their creative powers and were ourselves more aware of the range of their sensitivity and their gifts. Is this power a natural one to children, as it apparently was to Opal, and one which is all too quickly blunted and deadened by the adult world, where too many miss 'the many-splendoured thing'?

'Have you ever been walking in the country where you have stopped to look at the scenery? Can you imagine a fir tree and a sizal monkey tree, then a fawn tree? Then the bright rusty yellow leaves of the small trees down below and the sharp blades of grass glittering in the afternoon to six o'clock, and the red sky glowing through the branches, making shadows on the grass. It makes you want to stay and have a rest. As you walk along the grass you can hear it crunch as the dew comes, and when you sit down you fall asleep, for it is a land of glory.'

It has been suggested that Opal is of the company of Gilbert White, Darwin, Richard Jeffries and Fabre. Certainly the diary reveals someone with the Wordsworthian touch —

the earth
And common face of Nature spake to me
Rememberable things,

Wordsworth wrote,

and here is Opal, expressing the same thought:

'Every day now I do look for thoughts in flowers. Sometimes they are hidden away in the flower-bell — and sometimes I find them on a wild rose — and sometimes they are among the ferns — and sometimes I climb away up in the trees to look looks for them. So many thoughts do abide near unto us. They come from heaven and live among the flowers and the ferns, and often I find them in the trees.'

The discovery of a new wild flower gave her intense delight and satisfaction, the delight of a naturalist and a poet:

'I am joy all over. I have found in the near woods a plant that has berries like the berries symphorine has.'

To her everything lived with life as vivid as her own. She was intensely aware of the unity of life in all things and its continuity:

'Now are come the days of brown leaves. They fall from the trees. They flutter on the ground. When the brown leaves flutter they are saying little things. I hear them tell of their borning days when they did come into the world as leaves. Today they were talking of the time before their tree borning days of this spring-time. They told how they were a part of earth and air before their tree borning days. And now they are going back. In grey days of winter they go back to the earth again. But they do not die.'

15.

Inez Fortt put into words what many readers of the *Diary* feel:

'Whatever the truth of her claims, Opal Whiteley's life story holds an irresistible attraction for many people. I confess that I am one of them. I first learned of Opal during my college days in the 1920s. In English literature classes we read passages from her diary and discussed the beautiful imagery of her language. In the years since I have "lived" with Opal, "walked" the lonely forest paths with her, and read everything by and about her. It has been an obsession. I have talked with many who knew her in the early days and I have explored her childhood homes around Cottage Grove. I have corresponded with Opal. She was, and is, a most fabulous person, and I am sure will remain an enigma as well to most of us.'

Opal's 'wonderful world' is one she was only too happy to share with those who would listen. One who listened with intense fascination was Ida Wicks Schurtz of Eugene.

'Opal told beautiful stories,' said Mrs Schurtz. 'I know because I trailed after her in the woods. Opal was about 12 and I was around 6 or 7. It was pure joy to be with Opal. I have never forgotten my summers with her. To her I owe my love of nature. Through her I learned to see beauty in everything.

When Opal's book was published and she announced that she was not a Whiteley but the daughter of royalty, the family was deeply hurt. She looked exactly like all the Whiteleys with her beautiful dark brown expressive eyes. Though I don't know what to believe, I do know Opal would never deceive or lie. Whether her story is true or not, Opal believed in herself or she would not have announced she was of royal blood.'

The following letter came recently from the Hon. Mrs Woodruff. It was she who befriended Opal when she was in England and paid for the storage of her belongings when she went to hospital. She was one of the few who knew her as an adult.

'I first read the book when it came out when I was about 14. It made a deep impression on me at the time, but I never gave it another thought until over 20 years later I saw it in the house of friends ... when I commented on it my hostess said, "we were sorry for the poor little authoress who haunted Westminster Cathedral and was always so hungry." She always walked and never took a bus as far as one knew — whatever she had she spent on books.

In those days, 1935 or thereabouts, she was already talking about her Mother and Queen Marie making their baby clothes together, and her betrothal to the Prince of Wales — the abdication upset her terribly, and when it came to the coronation of George VI, we had her to stay with us in the country as it was feared she might make a public scene.

She refered (sic) to Aunt Maria (? illegible) the sister of Pius X, and made me think she had been looked after by her in early life — it was always difficult to know what was fantasy and what was true. She spoke of her Father as Prince Henry of Bourbon Orléans but I could never get her to tell me who the maman was. She made a number of different claims as to who her mother was: at one time an Austrian archduchess, at another a cousin of Prince Henry. She never seemed to be certain of her identity.' This is not as strange as it might appear. A young child knows its mother as 'mother' but may know nothing of her real name and position. If Françoise were taken away at an early age it is quite possible that she never knew who her mother was.

The letter goes on, 'She spoke with a slight American accent. The French Red Cross sought her out, acknowledging her French origin, and gave me a little subsidy for her. At last she became more strange so that neighbours complained that she ran out of the house at night calling for the Swami; I suppose some memory of her trip to India (she travelled with this 'holy man' in that country).

The authorities took her to hospital, where I visited her. I was not present when her possessions were removed from her rooms — there were books all round the walls in gin boxes which she bought from the local pub at 1p each.

I think a lot of her trouble was due to her never being loved, and a longing for a man. She used to tell me she had been affianced to all sorts of people — one was Averil Harriman, an American politician.'

References have been made to the existence of later diaries. When Ian Taylor was in America researching Opal's story for a television programme, he made a discovery of some material that had not come to light before. In the offices of the *Atlantic Monthly* he found ten typewritten pages, with notes in Opal's handwriting. There was a heading on the first page:

'About 9 years. summer-autumn 1907
AT CURTIN SPUR (DOUGLAS COUNTY).'

and the second section was headed:

'About 10 years. VAUGHANS SPUR
ROW RIVER CAMP.'

The contents bear the unmistakable imprint of Opal's personality, though it is clear that she is now older than when she wrote the original *Diary*. The fact that these are headed '9 years' and '10 years' would strengthen the evidence that the original *Diary* was written earlier, as she claimed. The same characteristics are evident: her delight in nature, her careful observation and her acceptance of her role as almost a servant in the Whiteley home. But now we meet her in another role — that of leader and teacher of the children, and we can understand how Mrs Schurtz felt about her.

We also meet some of her schoolfriends and can picture her in the schoolroom, carrying tadpoles in her dinner pail and getting her spelling wrong.

As we read these short pieces we cannot help wishing there had been more and hoping that possibly, one day, something more be found. This was written before the recent discoveries came to light from the Internet.

The nine year old *Diary* starts in late summer and autumn. Opal takes the children on a nature ramble:

'It is the time of goldenrod and the way is bordered with plumes of gold, bringing joy to the eyes of those who pass by. We children go unto them and watch the insects about them and upon them. We have this motto in our botany study: "Know the flowers and know their insect visitors." So every day new things we learn, and sweet the joy we find in knowing the everyday things around us.'

She causes trouble, as usual, in her eagerness to bring some inspiration into the home. The description of the sticky fir tree was surely written from experience:

'This has been quite a busy day. After part of the morning work was done the mamma and the children went a-visiting. I was left to mind the house, and told to stay and watch it all day. First I swept the floors and then I scrubbed them, then I started to clean the windows. I put bon ami all over those panes in the windows, then I made mottos — helpful things that Virgil and Horace and Seneca said in days of long ago — on the glass with my fingers. That gave the windows a proper look of inspiration, so I left the bon ami on — just as a background for the mottos. I gave the stove a good shine-up. Then I decided the house didn't need any more tending; it could take care of itself; so I latched the doors and went and gathered up a lot of the camp children to go on an exploration trip.

We walked along the flume and leaned over to pick leaves from the tops of the higher bushes. When we had gotten a goodly number of leaves, we played they were ships and sent them sailing down the flume with light cargoes laden. By-and-by we came to a very rocky place. A young fir tree was striving to grow up among all those rocks. It had a brave look. We children climbed down from the flume. We circled around that little tree and gave it our pledge of friendship. The children asked me to name it. I called it Theocritus because he said, "Who perseveres, succeeds at last." As we came away we noticed how cheery it looked and that it had a goodly number of pimples. Many young fir trees have pimples — as many as some people have freckles. These pimples are sticky — and bubbles of pitch with the skin stretched tight over them. They are very sticky and if one slides down a young fir tree that has pimples, one gets sticky all over.

As we went on we picked up rocks. They were mostly very hard rocks and some had streaks through them and some had little crystals inside them. Some were more heavy than others. When we had gotten a goodly number we started back to camp. We went around by the pond. We stopped at our beloved island Delos below the pond. We saw the water was drying up around it. Then that Delos might not develop into a peninsula and that it might continue as an island, we dug deeper the ditch around it and fixed a leakhole in the pond.'

The neighbours in the camp were mostly poor. One of them papered her bedroom with carefully hoarded newspapers.

'On the way to the old deserted house where I keep my Nature collections, we met Mrs Hanson. She was smiling a beaming smile. She was happy because she has her bedroom all papered new with clean newspapers. She has been saving them weeks unto the day she could paste them up — and now they are on the wall.'

Opal acted as teacher-nursemaid to the camp children but was not always welcomed by the parents.

'After we put the rocks away, we thought to go search for the Holy Grail. We went by to get little Harold. He so likes to go on searches for the Holy Grail. Then his mamma, Lela, would not let him go with us, Harold said a prayer word in not a prayer way and got his mouth washed out with soap.'

The incident of the death of Loralee's mother and the description of the logger, Sandy, is told with Opal's characteristic and unconscious skill.

'Then we went on down to the lower end of the camp to get Loralee. She was crying out by the chopping-block. Her mamma was just dead a few minutes before we got there — she was dead of typhoid fever. The doctor looked angry looks. He said everybody in camp must boil all water used for drinking and cooking. Too — he said — it was a wonder half the camp was not dead with typhoid fever.

We didn't linger to hear what else he had to say, because Jenny thought if we had the rope for Loralee to jump it would help to keep her from crying. She is so fond of jumping rope. We went over by the mill to get John to get the rope for us, but John wasn't there to get the rope for us. He has gone to catch one of the hired girls at another camp, who is running away with the husband of the sad lady who lives in the milltown and gave all we children ginger cookies one day when we were coming home from feeding earthworms to the baby birds; and being as John wasn't there to get the rope for Loralee to jump, I thought she would like to go for comfort to the cathedral, so we all went.

We had a short service. I didn't preach a very long sermon. We just sat still and listened to God's voice speaking to us through all the growing things around us. There were new flowers planted by the altar, and he who planted those new orchid tresses lovely by the altar in our cathedral was no other than Sandy, he who has as many freckles as the Milky Way has stars — he who used to work for Mortesson at Marquan — he who when comes pay-day gets so much whiskey out of bottles down his throat that he can hardly stand up and cannot keep on the proper tunes of the songs he sings at that time. All those orchid tresses he planted by the altar spoke of God's tender care for each flower, and we all know as God cares for the flowers and birds, so He cares for us.

From the Cathedral we went to the hospital, and there in the hospital to-day we were short of bandages, and after a short conference we amputated our apron strings, which made suitable bandages of assorted colors. When we arrived home near dark time our mammas, holding no conference, reached the unanimous decision that they would like to remove by surgical operation that part of our brains from which came the thought to amputate our apron strings. The switches left on the hazel bush by the window are few now.

The men being late coming home from work to supper, the mamma set me to mind the baby and the stew, that it did not boil over. While I was minding the baby and the stew, I carved a motto on the potato-masher. I carved it on so it wouldn't come off like chalk-marks, or the ones I made in the bon ami on the window that the mamma made me rub off. The motto I carved on the potato masher was what Plato said a long time ago about philosophy, "A striving after heavenly wisdom." Being as we have mashed potatoes every now and then, I can always take down that potato masher with a thrill. I am so fond of having mottoes around. They so give a helpful feel to the atmosphere when things get awfully hard, which is very often in a lumber camp. When the mamma came in to help me put supper on to the table and saw the potato masher with the motto carved on it, she said that I had caused it not to be a good potato masher any more, but I showed her where she was mistaken because every letter carved into that potato masher made it have more kinkles and more kinkles in a potato masher make it mash potatoes better.

But since supper-time I have found out something which I did not tell the mamma. I found that bits of potato stick in all those new kinkles the letters of the motto make, and that makes that potato masher lots harder to get clean. Why, it takes me three times as long to wash it with the motto on it as it did before I put that motto there. I really believe chalk mottoes are better after all on a potato masher.'

She writes of Angel Mother for the first time in this part of the diary. She and her sister sleep in a crib bed and the motherless child, Loralee is to share it that night.

'By-and-by, after I did get those dishes done up and put away, I went outdoors for the twilight hour with the camp children. They all sat in a row on the old log while I was telling them about Beethoven — telling them all I could remember of what my Angel Mother had told me a long time ago, and Loralee cuddled up close beside me. To-night she is going to sleep with Pearl and me in our crib bed.'

TEN YEAR OLD DIARY:

Opal does the housework before going to school. She has a problem with a stocking with a hole in it and dealing with that and numerous distractions on the way make her very late for school:

'This day I went forth into the forest at the hour of sunrise. And within the forest I heard a sublime, bell-like voice — 'twas one of his cathedral singers. Upward and onward the song of the little singer carried my soul — and nearer seemed the All-Wise Father as I stood there in the forest cathedral listening. He who in his singing lifts up the thoughts of the children of men to higher realms is this fairy, Audubon's Hermit Thrush. I could not linger to listen long. I had to get a hurry on me and get myself back to the kitchen, to put the coffee on and mix the griddlecakes and bake them for the papa's breakfast, and in between times to put up his lunch, for he has to be on his way to work before half-past six o'clock.

While I was making the cakes the bird song I heard in the cathedral sang on in my heart. It was a good start for the day.

After the papa went to work, the children and the mamma got up for breakfast. The mamma, not being hungry, did eat only two griddlecakes, but the children (who most of the time have appetites like unto those of young birds not out of the nest) did eat nineteen griddlecakes, which it did take some little time to bake. Then there were the chickens to feed. And there was milk to deliver. We get five cents a quart for milk. When these tasks were done I learned on inspection that there was not quite enough wood split up for the day.

When I was through splitting wood I sat down on the chopping-block to comb my hair for school. By the time the wood was in its proper place in the wood box back of the stove, it was near school time and I was in a pre dick a ment. Last eventide I was so busy with the nursery and the hospital that I did not get a certain hole in my stocking darned. The other holes didn't matter so much, but that particular hole did. It was a matter of importance because when I put that stocking on my foot that hole came in the same place where there was a hole in the shoe — right on the right foot where the little toe was. Its coming there made that little toe look like the littlest pig, that had to stay home on market-day but peeked out of the window. I couldn't take off the shoe to mend the stocking, as that would take too much time and would make me very late to school. So I went real quick to the cellar without the mamma knowing it, and gave that toe a good coating of liquid shoe-blacking. That made it look queer. It was ghastly gray. I knew that wouldn't do at all; so when the mamma wasn't looking, I took the stove blacking off the lamp shelf — and taking my dinner pail off the corner of the wood box, I hurried away to school.

On the way I saw twenty-one butterflies — seven Swallow-tails, nine Monarchs, three Checkerspots, a Painted Lady and Velvet Cloak. I spread my arms to sail along like all those butterflies, then I thought I had better hurry on to school. Pretty soon I found thirteen caterpillars and heard a Meadowlark sing three different songs, one after the other. Then I stopped at the Redwing Blackbird nursery. While I was there Father Blackbird, he with red upon his wings, came with a plump caterpillar and pausing a moment popped it into the wide-open mouth of Christopher Columbus and then was off again for another morsel. And I was off again for school. A little farther on I found seven more caterpillars — and in the pond by the great oak tree I found a goodly number of tadpoles. I took off my sun-bonnet and took my dinner out of the tin pail and put it into the sun-bonnet. Into the pail I put the tadpoles, then I hurried on to school.

When I did get to school I opened the door softly. I tiptoed into the cloakroom and hung my bonnet on its hook. I took the dinner pail with me to my seat, for I was afraid that something might happen to the tadpoles if I left them in the cloakroom. Just as I got to my seat teacher saw me. A lump came up in my throat and I gulped it down. Then I gave my apron a smooth out and was just going to sit down when he said, "Here — Opal — it's near recess and you should have been in school all morning."'

Opal turns on her charm and plans to explain why she was late.

'I swallowed another lump in my throat. Then I gave him a beaming smile and told him I would talk with him after spelling class. I thought then would be the proper time to tell him about all the things I saw and heard on the way to school this morning, because this is my day to be at the head of the class. And it would be quite thrilling to go from the head of the spelling class over to his desk and tell him all about it. I know I can do it in about two minutes. Then he will know why I didn't get to school in time, and why it is so much more interesting to go to school in the fields than to come to his school here.'

Among the papers I retrieved from the store in the East End of London there were two plain school exercise books, undated, and containing notes made in Opal's adult handwriting. These could be regarded as diaries, but they are quite different from both the early, published *Diary* and the recently discovered pages. There is none of the charm of the early writing. The freshness has gone and the quality that made the childhood diary so appealing.

Nonetheless they have interest, for the very fact that they are Opal's own writing, telling something of her life and thought, as she saw it, both in her early years and in the years between leaving the Whiteleys and her appearance in England. How much of what she describes actually happened is impossible to verify. One can only read what she wrote and draw one's own conclusions.

In one of them she wrote her memories of her childhood and later life, a remarkable account whatever the reader makes of it. She refers to 'H,' apparently another child, named Henri.

'REMEMBRANCE OF CHILDHOOD.

Remember Duke of Chartres dimly at seaside Cannes.

Maternal grandfather, Duke of Tuscany, who was fonder of F. (Françoise?) than his own little daughter Agnes who was only 6 years older. This accounts partly for the grand Duchess of Tuscany's hatred.

Grandmother Duchesse of Chartres at Chantilly, at Cannes (villa).

Remember father very distinctly teaching print alphabet birds, flowers, family history, lighting candles on birthdays.

Comparer, carrying on shoulders.

Remember mother in fields near Lindau & Salzburg (names given by mother) & lake near Lindau where Duke of Tuscany had house.

Florence with mother — sea — when father was in East & shortly before his death.

Also sea (Adriatic) on Duke of Tuscany's yacht. Mother there & ?

Remember Mother's maternal uncle a naturalist (a prince of Tuscany — bachelor) who spent 14 years in looking for

Françoise. Great love for her.

One day on lake Mother, brother, F. (Françoise) and others were out in boat on lake. Boat upset. F. (Françoise) & H. (Henri) separated from mother and told latter was dead. Mother told F. (Françoise) at Salzburg in Feb 1926 that she had been taken by force and orders of her mother to Salzburg. Accident happened after death of Prince Henri (1902?) to convince her mother that F. & H. had been drowned with a view to persuading her to marry a prince of Hohenzollern.' None of this is clear and these diary entries might foreshadow the confusion of Opal's mind which later became evident.

'F. & H. were taken to a wood where there were two big trees, situated near a gate on the estate of the Duke of Guise. Duchesse of Chartres told Françoise this in 1923. Here F. & H. were separated. At this time, an old governess in a poor house was with F. & H. A party attempted to kill F. & H. but governess protected children under table. F. saw her lying in blood on the floor. Duchess of Chartres told F. in 1923 that governess had then been murdered.

Vivid memories retained lumber camp — dream — the blood, the blood.

Never saw Henri after — ocean with strange people.

Duchesse de Chartres told F. that she thought the Duchesse de Guise instigated this trouble and actually struck the blow not with intention to kill. She was enceinte & very jealous of children because she loved prince Henri d'O and wished to marry him.

America — mining camp in California — Baker Co; Henry Pearson, a miner, gambling in San Francisco, remember gambling wheel, strangers.

Lumber camp with Whiteleys.'

The rest of the 'diary' tells of her time with the Whiteleys and at University.

Some of the entries in a second notebook may serve to throw light on the question of Opal's later experiences with men.

She never married, though she was attractive, intensely alive and strongly emotional and anxious to give and receive love. It may be significant that the 'relationships' in which she became involved were concerned, in three cases at least, with older men. In this she may have been seeking the father figure she missed in the death of Angel Father or in Mr Whiteley. The first was her publisher, George Palmer Putnam, who was engaged to and later married Amelia Earhart, the first woman to fly the Atlantic alone. Opal's feelings towards him were very strong and caused him embarrassment. She wrote to Constant Huntington:

'I do not understand my dear Mr Putnam marrying someone else when I love him so; *but I have faith that some day I will understand.*'

The second was a Roman Catholic priest, Father Bede Jarret. Her letters to him are very revealing and, again, caused much embarrassment. In the end she was barred from attending his church.

A correspondent, Miss Wheeler, wrote to me:

'I note a rather curious fact. It rather points to my own conclusion that she was psychic. I notice in the book that the name Bede occurs frequently: her American publisher was Elbert Bede (sic. In fact he was the editor of the Cottage Grove Sentinel). She had a pet sheep named Bede-of-Jarrow and when she was at Haverstock Hill she developed a tremendous devotion to the Provincial of the Dominicans, Fr Bede Jarret.

It was a quite harmless affair, just a spiritual romance on her side, as I think frequently happens with women in all churches. On his side it was a source of annoyance and irritation; he disliked women on the whole, in any case, and I understand be used to snub her.

When he died,' she went on, 'The Princess fell into an intensity of grief. The body lay in state in an open coffin and she lay prostrate on the ground beneath the coffin, which was on trestles. I incline to think that she is a genuine good person and *not* a fraud, her delusions, if they are delusions, are sincerely held. She may be one of those types, like Joan of Arc, who cannot be explained rationally. By her writing, she seems closer to nature than anyone I have ever read about. How then could she have endured living in London?'

The third was no other than Edward, Prince of Wales. She maintained that she had been promised 'as a child bride' to him and on the occasion of the coronation of George VI police protection was requested for her, in case she made a disturbance. The Home Office has a sizeable file of letters from her to 'Dear David.'

These were all situations in which there was no future, and there are two entries in the later diaries that may go some way to explaining this involvement in the impossible. They are:

'On recommendation of a Catholic priest F. (Françoise) rented a room from CL Aug 1918. Only there at night his son told F. he feared his father might harm her.

One evening F. noticed key of big salon door leading into her room was missing. She told the son, who was certain his father had taken it. (He) drove a large nail into the big cypress salon door. F. went to sleep but CL tried (the) salon door in night but could not force it. Next morning F. told Mrs L. who told F. that her husband had promised her never to molest F. F. said she would not stay another night in house. At 9 pm F. returned and went to bed.

Tues, woke to find CL holding her by her shoulders.

F. left 5 AM. Feb 1919 next day to a parent of children at Garvanza (who) found her an unfurnished room.'

The second concerned a Mr J. the grandfather of some children she had had in her Nature Classes — a man much respected. One afternoon Françoise went with him to meet the children and their mother who had gone for a walk along the beach. She went back and prepared dinner 'for 13. After dinner Mr J. made many proposals to F. but F, rushed out and hid in the sea the rest of the night behind pier posts. F, stayed in water 3 or 4 hours and returned after dawn unnoticed.

Frightened F. went to see Mrs T. who had always been her good friend. Mrs T. said that (J.) never harmed girls but only wanted to cuddle them.' Later 'Mr J, confronted with this, denied the incident and said she was an ungrateful little wench.'

Could this frightening experience have had the effect of directing the sexual feelings of this sensitive adolescent along paths where she would never be required to fully participate? We cannot say, but these simple entries have a ring of truth about them and, like so much of the rest of her writing, one finds it more difficult to believe that she made the whole thing up than if it actually happened.

16.

It is not surprising that Opal became suspicious as she grew older. She had reason. Her royalties from the *Atlantic Monthly* and from Putnam were not paid as they should have been; an article appeared in *The Queen* under her name — the one that I had found in the archives — which she had not in fact written. Its title was *Catherine the Great, the Greatest Hoax in History.* After some difficulty and the intervention of Constant Huntington the mistake was admitted. It turned out that the writer was at one time Editor of *The Queen.* He said, 'The reason that I used the name of the Princess Françoise de Bourbon-Orléans was because I was under the impression that this was a name invented in the office of *The Queen* to cover a series of articles written by an outside author in conjunction with a member of the office staff. The mistake is an unfortunate one, but I took every precaution before writing the recent article by looking up Bourbon-Orléans in the *Almanac de Gotha* and I did not find a possible Françoise. This confirmed my previous conviction that the name was a pseudonym.

I offer my sincere apologies to the Princess for any pain and annoyance I may have caused her by my misapprehension.'

Opal was then sent a cheque for five guineas 'without prejudice' in compensation.

There were hints in her later *Diary* and in letters that somebody was causing her fear — who, it is impossible to tell — but a letter written by a nun in a convent in Italy, warns her to leave the country without delay.

'I see that in Italy you are not safe. So do *exactly* what I tell you, for it is in your own interest. Leave Rome and go right out of Italy. Except for your papers you must keep your incognito, Loraine. D'O ... is not safe. As soon as you are in Austria I will write and explain you all about it. Now I cannot do so. Do not return here now. It would not be safe. Tear up this note.'

Wherever she went she seemed to arouse intense feelings of loyalty and affection, and the opposite. Some of her so-called friends and befrienders quickly cooled off and discarded her. They accused her of being a fraud and an imposter. Others gave her endless support. Her English publisher, Constant Huntington, in particular, showed unfailing patience and caring, well beyond the bounds of the publisher-author relationship. His frequent letters, though hinting at the problems she presented him with, never deviated from kindness and support.

He kept her boxes of books and the few pieces of furniture she possessed in the firm's warehouse and arranged for delivery and collection of her personal belongings in her many moves from place to place.

He negotiated for her with other publishers in attempts to get her work placed and to get her rights recognised.

She was welcomed and taken care of in a number of convents and in private homes, but all the time she was in fact alone. That no one really believed her claims must have been distressing, whether or not the facts were true, and as one after another rejected her it is not surprising that she became suspicious and difficult.

The only other publication that has come to light is a small volume of verse which she published herself, in 1923. She called it *The Flower of Stars*. The poems have a haunting quality and reveal the writer as someone living in a strange dream world of imagination and feeling, striving to express thoughts that are probably inexpressible, and aware of suffering and sorrow. Some may see in them the hint of the imbalance that developed in her later life. Others may think of poets who equally lived on the edge of madness yet expressed truth as the sane cannot do.

BEAUTY ATTENDS.
Beauty attends the birthing of Man,
And she attends his death.
The white altar fires
Of her high hopes
Are then a little dimmed.
Sometimes, they are almost gone out.

THE LITTLE ROOM.
In Man's heart
Is a little room.
He has named it
Oblivion.
And things are ranged along its wall
That he does not wish
To think about.
Every time that he pushes something in there
He closes the door very tightly.
But in hours when he is weary,
In the hours that walk around some midnights
When high fires have burned
To a low flicker
Then the little door swings on its hinges.
And no thing
Will make it stay closed
All of the time.

When he is near death
All the Velvet-footed Wanderers in there

Join the throng around his bed.
'We will not die,' they whisper
To one another.
While beauty waits with drawn lips
and dry eyes.
But, there is heard
The patter of a little sad rain
In her heart's garden
Where some little flower buds
That were once thinking of the sun
Will never open
Because man keeps a little room
Of oblivion in his soul.

ALL THINGS LIVE

All things live;
The innermost thoughts
Of a Man's soul
Walk the highway
Of the Universe,
And are seen
By all the pilgrims,
Who have gone before.

Ellery Sedgwick, in a letter to Constant Huntington, gave some remarkable information, said to have come to him through Mr Whiteley. It appears that he had received certain letters which 'were all typewritten, and the writer was ill at ease in using English, though whether he was a foreigner or uneducated, would be hard to tell — probably both. At any rate, they combined to support with extraordinary circumstantial detail Opal's complete story. They asserted that Mrs Whiteley had agreed to receive the new Opal for the sum of 10,000 francs; that the instalments of this money had not been regularly paid; that Mrs Whiteley had intended to devote it to providing handsomely for her daughters, and that before her death in 1917 she had requested that, when the money had been paid, it should be invested in a series of presents for her daughters and for Mr Whiteley. In conformity with this wish, so the writer said, the money, which had been paid was invested and the proceeds duly forwarded. They included a gold watch and a silver shaving-mug for Mr Whiteley, and for the two daughters a very long and curious list of silverware, totaling 21 pieces.'

'I have been informed,' Sedgwick concluded 'that these pieces have arrived.'

One can only speculate on the 'evidence' contained in this report and its source.

Sedgwick went on:

'During the month of March (I believe) a new element was injected into the drama by a certain Mrs Duane, who had lived in France, near Chantilly. She had read the diary with immense interest, sought Opal's acquaintance, noticed a real or fancied resemblance to a child and her mother walking in the park at Chantilly — two figures which in those days left an enduring impression upon her. Returning to the diary, Mrs Duane noticed frequent references to features of the local topography, familiar to her through extended residence — St Firmin, the brook Nonette, the Route de Connétable, etc., etc. The detailed knowledge shown by the diarist seemed extraordinary. Discovery led to discovery, and one day she (Françoise?) telephoned to me that she had a clue.

That this clue is genuine so far as the textual references in the diary go, there is not the smallest doubt. The diarist declares in so many words that her Angel Father was born in the Morgan House at Ham on October 15th, 1867; that her grandpère was on the staff of General McClellan in the United States and he served with General Saussier in Africa; that aunts, uncles and other progenitors are none other than those distinguishing the family of prince Henri of Orleans, the famous explorer and scientist who died in Saigon in 1901.

I will not take your time to cite the evidence in regard to the identification of the events in Prince Henri's life, — (what a pity!) — but will content myself with saying that the testimony is overwhelming. The dates, of course, synchronize both with the incident of the lady described by Mrs Duane and with Opal's own story of her early years.' The reader can only be immensely frustrated by Sedgwick's omission.

The letter goes on, 'I do not want to give you the impression that this extraordinary story burst upon me all at once. It came little by little, a bit here, a bit there. It did not seem wise to tell Opal. I did tell her that if she insisted, I would show her all my evidence, but when once she knew, further revelations from the diary would, for obvious reasons, have far less weight.'

Presumably he was here referring to the discovery of the acrostics or anagrams in the diary, which spelled the names of Opal's supposed Angel Father and Mother and others of her relatives.

It seems that it was from this time that Opal's suspicions of Sedgwick dated and she engaged a lawyer, who, however, did not press the case. At the end of the summer, Sedgwick reported, after she had spent time as a governess with friends of the Sedgwicks at Beverley, Massachusetts, 'Opal left suddenly for New York in the company of some mysterious visitors who arrived for her, deep in the country at eleven o'clock in the night. Her affairs are now in the hands of lawyers who write to my counsel, "You do not realise the intensity of feeling on the part of Miss Whiteley's advisers in New York. I do not think you realize the seriousness of the situation."

The significance of this is still beyond my comprehension,' Sedgwick continued. 'It is possible that Opal believes I am standing between her and a great inheritance. It is also possible she thinks I have discovered some evidence of apparent proof of duplicity. There is in my files a mass of evidence on the general story.'

How much one wishes this evidence were available.

Huntington replied to this letter, 'Please believe me that I very warmly appreciate your frankness in writing to me so fully. All that you say, however, makes me more than ever glad to be associated with this fascinating book, and I am proportionately grateful to you for introducing it to me. I have no doubt that Lord Grey will take the same view when he reads your letter.'

In a subsequent letter he wrote:

'I shall look out for the article about Miss Whiteley's parentage in the April *Bookman.* I wonder if this will deal with the extraordinary anagrams? These, of course, have the greatest interest, and I suppose they are sooner or later sure to be discovered and reported in the press. For the present however, I understand that Miss Whiteley and her representatives do not wish any such announcement to be made.'

In April 1930, Huntington wrote to the Putnam Syndicate in New York in connection with Opal's account of her journey to India and the book she was hoping to publish, *The Sun King*.

'The Princess is very anxious indeed to secure some sort of an arrangement and she hopes that you will try all the possible papers in the order of the terms they are prepared to pay. You can make the most of her authorship of *The Story of Opal Whiteley* and the fact that she has now assumed the position as a member of the French royal family, as foreshadowed by the acrostics in *The Story of Opal.* She does not wish to start a controversy as many of her relatives are hostile but there would seem to be no harm in telling any editor privately that certain members of the family have accepted her and that her passport is made out in the name of Françoise Marie de Bourbon-Orléans.'

Would the editor of a respected publishing house recommend that these 'facts' could be given to editors if there were serious doubts about their authenticity?

Constant Huntington and his wife and daughter visited Françoise at Emperor's Gate, London, in 1929. He wrote:

'Gladys and I and Alfreda went to call on Sunday afternoon and found her in an attic room at the top of a Roman Catholic women's club. She had her entire walls covered with French royalist coats-of-arms (which she said used to hang in the house of her father, Prince Henri d'Orléans) and miniatures of the family of Bourbon-Orléans. Gladys, who knows history like a book, recognised a great many of them and the princess knew all the names and the genealogy perfectly.'

Others had seen and been impressed by the miniatures and pictures. A friend wrote to Françoise in 1923. She addressed her as 'Dear Princesse' and says:

'I wonder whether you would lend your beautiful pictures and miniatures as a 'loan collection' to the Victoria and Albert Museum? They would be safe there as at the Bank, and would be beautifully taken care of. I was *amazed* at the *gems* you possess in those portraits and miniatures and I was so much interested. Thank you for giving me so great a treat in showing me your treasures.'

A letter written to Françoise in 1921 or 1922, from a man who called himself 'Fairy Godfather' accused her of being unable or unwilling to look at her own faults. 'I had hoped,' the letter read, 'to find in you a real desire to improve and to get rid of your faults. The child of the *Diary* has been 'overlaid;' but the child of the *Diary* is still alive and deep down in your heart she is still a possibility. One of the things we want to do for you is to help you get rid of these 'layers' which conflict with the world has deposited all over you, and which so often conceal the most dear child of the *Diary*. It is because we believe in and love that child, that we are willing to try so hard on your behalf.' Just what this referred to it is impossible to say, but reading a number of letters from this individual one gets the impression of an overbearing and insensitive influence, possibly of a narrow evangelical character. He called her 'naughty' although she was by then a young woman of twenty-four, and he seemed to show little understanding of a growing adolescent which at that stage she really was. He goes on, 'We are always unhappy, we always suffer when we are bad,' and his letter ends, 'I want you to pray for light and guidance and then to write me what you think.'

Ellery Sedgwick wrote of this 'friend' of Opal:

'This man has, it seems, been very successful in business, and at fifty, finds himself in retirement with a deep religious interest in good works. He has built, or endowed, a chapel on the East side in New York, and over this chapel has his bachelor quarters. He was evidently ripe for a romantic adventure and Opal's cause made a complete knight errant of him. He apparently had taken up the cudgels on her behalf in a disagreement with her publishers.'

The letter — to Constant Huntington — goes on to say that Opal is living with a Mrs Griscom, 'widow, I believe, of the late ambassador to Germany. She is treated *en princesse,* and not allowed to be alone day or night. (Opal had reported, in relation to her stay with this family, that she had been kept a prisoner. This may have been the source of Sedgwick's information.)

A letter from Mrs Miller, whose daughter Opal had been engaged to teach, shows a little more understanding of Opal's complex character and what she had been through. The letter says:

'You write about brooding inside yourself and how this gets you into mix ups, it is so easy to see how this habit has grown on you, how it started, probably way back in the lumber camp, because there was no one to go to, no one to trust.'

Mrs Griscom called herself 'Fairy Godmother.' Clearly she had a deep affection for Opal, in spite of the trials that she seemed to cause. She wrote, in September 1920:

'I have missed you so much since you went away. A week from today and you will be back again and as you say not for parting. That is a beautiful thought to me.

I should like to find out your Angel father's name and as much as possible.' And in another letter, undated, she wrote: 'We are all so happy things are going so beautifully so far, and to think you are going to be here sooner even than we had planned. It is beautiful. I am so happy over it all. It is one of the truest most beautiful fairy stories ever known.'

In spite of this Opal was still accused of not telling the truth. Another letter from 'Fairy Godfather' read:

'I wish you would please do as I asked, and would tell me briefly the 6 biggest lies you can remember.'

He did give a reason for her telling lies and in so doing appeared to show some understanding. She had wished to go to Hollywood but had denied the fact and her 'Fairy Godfather' wrote:

'There was nothing "awful" about your having wished to appear in motion pictures. It was wrong and foolish to have lied about it. I had guessed that you had wanted to appear in the movies and that you had denied it from false shame. Nearly all the lies you have told have been of the same kind — fear of being misjudged if you had told the truth.' And in another equally well-meaning and misguided letter:

'The first step is to recognise the existence of faults — of self-will and vanity and conceit and resentment and jealousy and self-pity, and so forth. The fourth step is to be sorry for your faults simply because they offend God and because they add terribly to the burden which Christ has to carry.' One can only guess how this kind of reaction may have piled up an unbearable sense of guilt in Opal's mind.

There was much more in this vein, exposing Opal's 'sins.' Her 'Fairy Godfather' appeared to have been acting as God, and an Old Testament God at that. He writes of helping her to overcome the evil in her nature and one wonders what inner conflicts he was trying to cover up in himself by his self-righteous preaching. Opal may well have been all that he accused her of, but there was no one in her circle who recognised her behaviour as a cry for help. How did they think she would take such a frontal attack, so devoid of real understanding and love?

17.

Before we leave the question of the truth of Opal's claim that she was not a Whiteley, two small points should be mentioned, which may or may not be of any significance. A friend of mine, who was a clairvoyant was handling a photograph of Opal, whom she had never seen, and about whom she knew nothing. She said:

'This person comes from America. I get a forestry camp. Her parents were unkind to her. She was beaten. Her mother put her under the table. I get Austrian and German connections.'

I then told her more about Opal. She then said:

'If you reverse the name, "Opal," you get "lapo" — the initials of "la Princesse d'Orléans."'

There is no doubt that there was a feeling of antipathy in the community towards the strangely different child. She had few companions and lived a life apart. When I was in Oregon I spoke to an audience of about a hundred in Eugene University, some of whom had known her when they were children. They told me that when she went past their homes, their mothers called them in, for they believed she was a witch. At the end of my talk, one of the audience came up and thanked me, and said:

'You have dispelled the myths and misconceptions of the community.'

Ever since I first read her diary, I had had the wish to go to

Oregon, to see where she had lived, and to meet the people who had known her. It was sixty years before I was able to carry out this wish and I felt that this remark made it all worth while.

Interest in Opal and her *Diary* is still very much alive in America. The following appeared on the Internet and was e-mailed to Lynne Anderson-Inman by Steve Williamson in August 1999. In the context of Opal's story it appears of very great interest.

'Here is an e-mail about an exiled French priest in 1903. He was both in Colton, Washington, and down near Wendling (about 30 miles).

If Opal — or some child — was sent to the US from France — this priest — or someone like him would have been a good person to send the child with and Colton, Washington, and Booth Kelly Lumber would have been the perfect place to do it.

I found the grave of a priest in the nuns' cemetery at St Gertrude's convent. He was the lone male buried among all the nuns. I wanted to get more information on him before I wrote to you. It may be a lead to the "angel father" of Opal's.

He was Father Marchard. He and his monks were exiled from France, because of their political sympathies with the Royal family. He visited the Benedictine nuns in Colton while looking for a place to establish his own monastery. Abbot Marchard had to flee France in 1903. His monastery was closely tied to the French aristocracy and it was ordered closed by the government. The abbot and a few monks fled to Oregon. Their abbey in France was near Lyons and Orleans. It had close ties to both French and British royalty. Abbot Marchard and his group wandered around Portland and Washington for two years. For some reason the Abbot and his group had very hard financial times in Oregon and they broke up. The Abbot went to work with the Benedictine nuns at St Scolastica's in 1911. He and his monks ran a saw mill near the town of Wendling.

I need to find out more about Abbot Marchard's moves in Oregon and Washington. I have always thought that there would be someone in Opal's background who knew the Orleans family and was connected to them.

Father Marchard's abbey was strongly connected to the St Lazarus hospitals. The Green Cross was headquartered in France, and also included members of many European Royal houses. Many of them came to America in the anarchist's uproar of the early days of this century (the nineteenth). The Orleans family in France and Belgium gave large sums of money to a diocese in Walla Walla, Washington (very near Colton) in 1847 and later in the 1800s. It would have been Prince Henri's grandfather who began this.'

More evidence of a link between the Orleans Royal family and Oregon appears in further research in the Internet carried out by Steve Williams. Apparently the logging company, Booth Kelly, had offices in Mexico, where in the late 1800's there was a member of the Orleans family as 'king.' Steve Williams reports that Oregon has many French names for towns, including an old abandoned town named Orleans, which is now nothing but a small cemetery; it was a high French Catholic area.

'None of this,' Steve Williams says, 'is conclusive proof of anything except a circumstantial case that Oregon and Washington were more French than people ever realized and that this area would have made a safe haven from the problems in Europe and Asia in 1900.'

'This information, appearing as it has at the eleventh hour, cannot but be of the greatest interest, confirming my belief and that of others closely involved in Opal's story, that some such knowledge might, in time, come to light.

Two more e-mails, of remarkable interest, were sent to Lynne Anderson-Inman by Steve Williams:

'I may have found a fragment from one of Opal's diaries. I am having a woman at Cottage Grove compare the handwriting to Opal's. The handwriting is much like Opal's.

Inside a 1905 book I noticed a fragment of paper carefully tucked inside another piece of paper. The book also had trillium flowers pressed into it. It is one quarter of an 8/11 page — torn... It was clearly torn on purpose — and this one fragment preserved inside the book. It is not dated — but is very old. The paper was torn — it did not break into fragments because of age. Someone also tried to burn it according to the expert who is now reviewing it.

It is a fragment from someone's diary — written in a composition book — by a girl — near a mill and a river — and she writes about gathering flowers, encountering a snake and a deer. The girl would likely be a young teen — and one who had attended school.

As you know, Opal always maintained that her sister tore up the diary when Opal was 12 and the family lived at Star. This piece of paper has NEVER been in Los Angeles or Boston — it could not have been "made up" later. And it is clear that it was deliberately torn into quarters. It has probably not been out of that book in nearly 100 years. It would strongly support that Opal did keep a diary and it was torn up as she claimed.

So, right now, what we have is a quarter page of a girl's diary that a neighbour of Opal and her family carefully preserved in a big old book. It rested there — along with trillium flowers for over 90 years — until a Mrs Slater came to 100th anniversary party for the Dorena Post Office hoping to find a local group to give the book to.

It is from two one-quarter pages. Also, the first word or two is missing from each sentence — likely it was torn from the composition book and then torn twice again.

Note the words Fairy, Lizzie, mill, river, deer. Also, it is a very long shot, but Faye Whiteley's name means 'fairy or elf' in French and Latin — it may have been a nickname.

Note also that she begins the entry 'Dear Composition' — she is writing TO the composition Book — like 'Dear Diary.'

There is a piece in the *Atlantic Monthly* that quotes Opal as saying that she wrote in an old 'composition book.' (I have two of these in my possession, and there is one in the archives of the University of London Library — author).

18.

The story of Opal — difficult to believe and yet impossible to dismiss — is unfinished. The mystery baffles still. There are many questions that will probably never be answered and many problems which may always be unsolved. The more one ponders on the diary the deeper the tangle grows, and one's mind repeatedly swings from scepticism to conviction and back again. So much that seems inexplicable, so many improbabilities, are interwoven with what is recognized immediately as truth in this fascinating and apparently insoluble jigsaw puzzle.

S L Bensusan believed that Opal's *Diary* should be described as a great work. He wrote,

'There are many definitions of a work of art but whether it takes the form of a picture, a piece of music, a statue or indeed any other expression of a gifted being's temperament, there is at least one simple test of quality that may be applied. If it makes life appear more beautiful, if it deepens our sense of gratitude for what has been given to us in overflowing measure, then it is a great work. Now it is impossible for any reader with an instinct for, and a response to, natural beauty to rise from the perusal of Opal, Whiteley's diary without feeling a quickened sense of gratitude for the good and simple things of life. No sophisticted writer or thinker could have moved a reader of average mentality so deeply. Opal because she could write her thoughts down without self-consciousness, has charmed a multitude and set many of them looking wistfully for what they have forgotten too long.'

There is no doubt at all that Opal, through her *Diary,* brought some of the colour and freshness of spring into the greyness of our days and gave us a new understanding of childhood. This was her gift to us; by this she will be remembered, for she made many of us look at the world around with clearer eyes and left us richer for having known her. Who the author of the *Diary* really was and what were the circumstances of her life — neither of these is of great importance. What matters intensely is the insight which her writing gives into the feelings of a child, at an age when most children are still inarticulate and incapable of such self-revelation. Whether it was based on fact or fantasy, the *Diary* is still a unique record of the inner life of a sensitive child, made when the dew was still on the grass, of one who knew

> Earth's crammed with heaven,
> And every common bush aflame with God:
> But only he who sees takes off his shoes.